THE —— UNEXPLAINED

HISTORIC REALMS
OF MARVELS AND MIRACLES

Produced by Carlton Books Limited
20 Mortimer Street
London, W1N 7RD

Text and Design copyright © Carlton Books Limited 2001

First published in hardback edition in 2001 by Chelsea House Publishers, a subsidiary of
Haights Cross Communications. Printed and bound in Dubai.

First Printing
1 3 5 7 9 8 6 4 2

The Chelsea House World Wide Web address is http://www.chelseahouse.com

Library of Congress Cataloging-in-Publication Data applied for

Historic Realms of Marvels and Miracles ISBN: 0-7910-6076-4
Ancient Worlds, Ancient Mysteries ISBN: 0-7910-6077-2
Lost Worlds and Forgotten Secrets ISBN: 0-7910-6078-0
We Are Not Alone ISBN: 0-7910-6079-9
Imagining Other Worlds ISBN: 0-7910-6080-2
Coming from the Skies ISBN: 0-7910-6081-0
Making Contact ISBN: 0-7910-6082-9

THE UNEXPLAINED

HISTORIC REALMS
OF MARVELS AND MIRACLES

Between Myth and Materiality

Dr Karl P.N. Shuker

Chelsea House Publishers

Philadelphia

THE UNEXPLAINED

HISTORIC REALMS
OF MARVELS AND MIRACLES

Ancient Worlds, Ancient Mysteries

Lost Worlds and Forgotten Secrets

We Are Not Alone

Imagining Other Worlds

Coming From the Skies

Making Contact

CONTENTS

'Twixt Heaven and Earth, Present and Past

The Holy Thorn and the Holy Grail

William Blake's immortal poem and hymn, "Jerusalem", refers to the possibility that as a boy Jesus visited Great Britain, with his tin-trading uncle, St Joseph of Arimathea. There are also stories of how, after the death of Jesus, St Joseph travelled to Britain again, founding a small church at Glastonbury in Somerset. Destroyed by fire in 1184, this was replaced by the abbey, which was razed by King Henry VIII in 1539 but whose ruins stand today.

Glastonbury, of course, has an additional claim to mythological fame, for some historians believe it to be the Isle of Avalon, to which King Arthur was taken to be healed when mortally wounded in his last battle. In fact, Glastonbury has been the focus of some intricate interweaving of Arthurian and Christian romances, as will be seen.

According to legend, while St Joseph was at Glastonbury his staff rooted in the ground and burst forth into a great thorn tree. Here too, in the church's well, St Joseph reputedly concealed the Holy Grail – the chalice that Jesus drank from during the Last Supper, and which was used to catch drops of his blood falling from his crucifixion wounds.

So much for legend, but does any of it have a basis in fact? There was indeed a large thorn tree in the grounds at Glastonbury, but puritanical Oliver Cromwell ordered it to be cut down, condemning it as an idolatrous

Detail of window in Kilkhampton parish church, Devon: Joseph of Arimathea carrying the Holy Thorn and the Holy Grail.

image. In 1985, however, one of its descendants was planted on this same spot; others can be found elsewhere in the abbey grounds. Interestingly, their subspecies, *Crataegus oxyacantha praecox*, is not native to Britain, but is found in the Holy Land – support, perhaps, for the legend of St Joseph's journey to Britain?

The history of the Holy Grail is far more complex, confusing and contradictory. Many historians nowadays consider that its Christian associations, so familiar today, are actually a relatively recent invention, and that the real source of the Holy Grail concept can be traced much further back in time than Christianity – as far back as the distant realms of Celtic mythology. Here it is equated with a magic cauldron owned by the god Bran that could restore to life anyone whose slain body was cast into it.

In *The Shroud and the Grail*, Noel Currer-Briggs proposed that there were two separate Grails that have since become confused with each other. One is the chalice that we generally think of today as the Holy Grail. However, the other, which he believes to be the true Grail, was the dish-shaped reliquary casket that had contained the linen sheet wrapped around the body of Jesus after he was removed from the cross, i.e. the Shroud of Turin.

No less conflicting are the many Arthurian tales of the quest for the Grail, believed to possess great healing powers. In the most famous of these, Sir Thomas Malory's *Le Morte Darthur* (1485), the quest was achieved jointly by Sir Galahad (Gawain in some other tellings), Sir Perceval and Sir Bors, who reached the Grail Castle, surrounded by a barren wasteland, to find that the holy chalice was guarded by a wounded,

La Mort d'Arthur by James Archer.

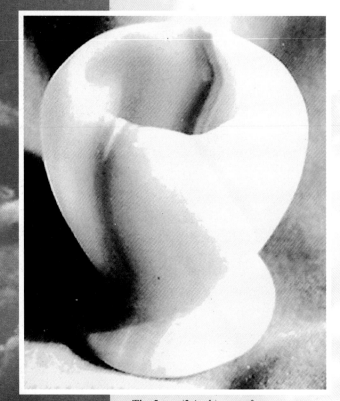

The 5-cm (2-inch) cup of green onyx believed by Dr Graham Phillips to be the legendary Holy Grail used to collect the blood of Jesus.

immobile keeper, the Fisher King. Only when a certain question relating to the Grail is asked correctly can the Fisher King be healed, the land restored and the Grail obtained. Sir Galahad successfully posed the question, and the trio of knights then transported the Grail by ship to a holy Eastern city called Sarras, where Galahad was crowned king before Perceval returned to the Grail Castle and Bors to Camelot. The Grail's subsequent fate, however, became obscured by countless claims of conspiracies, intervention by the Knights Templar, Cathars and so on.

A very different history has been mooted by the author Dr Graham Phillips in his latest work *The Search For the Grail*. He believes that the Holy Grail was removed from the tomb of Jesus in AD 327 by archaeological scholars sent by the Roman empress Helena, and taken back with them to Rome. In 410, when Rome was under attack from barbarian hordes, the Grail was smuggled out, sent to Britain, which was still under Roman occupation, and placed for safety in the city of

Viroconium, in what is today the county of Shropshire. Here it came under the protection of a local king, whom Phillips believes to have been none other than King Arthur, and remained undisturbed for several centuries, until the Norman invasion, when Arthur's lands – and the Grail – were given to Payn Peveril, a French nobleman.

From then on, the Grail was passed down through successive generations of the Peveril family. In 1850, his last direct descendant, Frances Vernon, married a local historian called Thomas Wright, but their only child, a son, died while still a youngster. What would become of the Grail now? Wright and his wife decided to conceal their precious heirloom. Nevertheless, Wright was concerned that the Grail might be lost forever and so he left behind some cryptic clues to its location – an artificial cave in Hawkstone Park near Shrewsbury – appended to a poem relating to the Grail written by one of his wife's ancestors in the seventeenth century.

After Thomas Wright's death, his wife remarried, and in 1920 one of her grandchildren, Walter Langham, learnt about his family's connection with the Grail. Deciphering Wright's clues, Langham trekked through a maze of tunnels and caves beneath the White Cliff, a ruined chapel at Hawkstone Park. And there, hidden beneath a stone eagle, he discovered a 5-cm- (2-inch) tall goblet hewn from green onyx and very worn. Could this really be the Holy Grail?

Experts are presently nonplussed, and because the goblet is composed of onyx its age cannot be ascertained by carbon dating. Regardless of its identity, however, why had its existence not been made public before now? After Langham found it, the goblet remained in his family, but when it passed into the hands of its current owner, Langham's great-grand-daughter Victoria Palmer, living in Rugby in Warwickshire, she was wholly unaware of its controversial claim to fame. Indeed, until Phillips contacted her in 1995 to tell her that it might actually be the Holy Grail, since when she has consigned it to the safety of a bank vault – it had been residing inside a box of junk in her attic! How very unromantic an end to the history of what may be one of the world's most inspirational religious artefacts!

THE LITTLE PEOPLE

One day in July 1917, 15-year-old Elsie Wright took her father's box camera to a woodland glen in Cottingley, Yorkshire, and took her very first photograph: it became one of the most famous, and controversial, images ever exposed to public scrutiny. For the photograph depicted her 10-year-old cousin Frances Griffiths with a group of diminutive winged fairies, dancing in front of her. Two months later, the two girls obtained a second photo, this time portraying Elsie with a gnome. These extraordinary pictures greatly intrigued theosophist Edward Gardner, and they fascinated Sir Arthur Conan Doyle, who was preparing a book called *The Coming of the Fairies* (published in 1922) and was naturally eager to pursue any evidence that might confirm the reality of such entities. As a result, the two girls were given fresh cameras and photographic plates and asked to take some more fairy photos, which in August 1920 they did – three in all. In the last of these the fairies were semi-transparent, as if fading from view, and Elsie claimed that she could not photograph them any more.

For 57 years, this quintet of pictures perplexed the scientific world. Although Elsie and Frances repeatedly swore that they were genuine, most people felt sure that they were fakes and it was well known that Elsie had always been an accomplished painter, but not even photographic experts were able to show how the hoax had been perpetrated. In August 1977, however, writer Fred Gettings solved the mystery. Looking through a children's book called *Princess Mary's Gift Book*, published in 1915 and widely available at that time, he spotted some fairy illustrations that were virtually identical to the fairies in Elsie's first picture.

An account of his discovery appeared in *The Unexplained* (No. 116) in 1982, but the next issue contained an even more sensational coup – an article by fairy researcher Joe Cooper claiming that Elsie and Frances had admitted to

Fairies in flight, with "… the Moon, like to a silver bow/New-bent in Heaven", and Titania, Queen of the Fairies, lying asleep. Arthur Rackham's illustration (1908) for William Shakespeare's **A Midsummer Night's Dream**.

him that they had indeed hoaxed the pictures, using cut-out fairies painted by Elsie. The long-running saga finally came to an end on 17 March 1983, when Frances confessed to *The Times*, which published the news the next day, with a confirmation by Elsie appearing in its issue of 4 April.

Full details of how Elsie and Frances had accomplished the deed were revealed in a comprehensive series of *British Journal of Photography* articles by Geoffrey Crawley, running from 24 December 1982 to 8 April 1983. Perhaps the most remarkable revelation in the Cottingley exposé, however, was that a major clue to the pictures' true nature

had been clearly visible all along. Some of the cut-outs had been held in place by hatpins, and the head of one pin had been noticed by Conan Doyle but identified by him as a fairy navel!

Notwithstanding the demise of these photos as evidence for the reality of fairies, modern-day sightings of the Little People in Britain still occur. In 1928, Mrs G. Herbert recollected seeing a pixie while taking an afternoon walk on the southern edge of Dartmoor as a child in 1897. It resembled a little wizened man about 45 cm (18 inches) tall with a brown wrinkled face and wearing a pointed hat, doublet and knicker-like leggings. As she looked at

The Cottingley fairies: one of Elsie Wright's controversial photographs.

it, the pixie vanished. A similar being was briefly spotted in April 1936 by a car driver when rounding a bend along a quiet Hertfordshire lane.

An unnamed correspondent in the periodical *John o'London's* (June 1933) claimed that on eight occasions during August 1931, she and her eldest daughter had spied some 45-cm- (18-inch) tall female fairies wearing delicate transparent gowns in their Warwickshire garden. Around August 1887 or 1888, teenager Grace Penrose saw three small doll-like figures in identical white gowns, dancing by a well behind her home at Sennen Cove, Cornwall. More recently, during summer 1964, some children claimed that they had watched a number of little green men in white hats hurling stones and clods of earth at each other on a bowling green in Liverpool.

Most bizarre of all, however, must surely be the statement made by a group of 10-year-old children that while walking home from Wollaton Park, Nottingham, one evening in late September 1979, they saw a troupe of about 60 gnomes drive out of the lakeside bushes in 30 tiny red and white bubble cars! The gnomes were described

as being only half as tall as the children themselves, with greenish crinkled faces, red tunics, green leggings, and white beards with red tips. Despite rigorous questioning the following morning by their school's headmaster, the children insisted that they were telling the truth. Marjorie Johnson, a former secretary of the Fairy Investigation Society based in Nottingham, disclosed that she had received several other reports of Little People from Wollaton Park, often near to its lake.

Identities proposed for the Little People are numerous. Traditionally they have been deemed to be lost souls or the souls of pre-Christian people, doomed to wander the earth until they ultimately disappear. Others consider them to be fallen angels, or elemental nature spirits inhabiting a different dimension of reality from our physical world, or even visible thought-forms – mentally projected *à la* Ted Serios, America's foremost "thoughtographer".

Some researchers, noting that the overall decline in modern-day fairy reports is matched by the contemporary surge in UFO sightings, suggest that fairies may have abandoned dancing in

secluded groves in favour of soaring through the skies in flying saucers. Certainly, encounters with fairies and supposed extraterrestrials do share many similarities.

In 1893, folklorist David MacRitchie expressed the opinion that the Little People were the last remnants of a pygmy race of ancient Britons, and Neolithic pygmies have been nominated as the answer to continental Europe's fairies too. Recalling Dr Carl Sagan's theory that humankind's longstanding belief in dragons stems from archaic racial memories, persisting through millions of years from prehistoric times when the earliest mammals co-existed with dinosaurs, I cannot help but wonder if the Little People are racial memories of our more direct ancestors, the dwarf-like australopithecines, which died out around one million years ago. As all races of *Homo sapiens* are descended from these, this would explain the worldwide belief in Little People.

Even so, the fundamental question is not what the Little People are, but whether they exist. Or to put it another way, in the words of J. M. Barrie: "Do you believe in fairies?"

CROSSE'S ACARI

The author Mary Shelley once attended a lecture in London given by an eccentric electrical researcher from Somerset called Andrew Crosse. Traditionally, the inspiration for her classic horror story, *Frankenstein*, is believed to have been a nightmare, but in his intriguing book *The Man Who Was Frankenstein*, writer Peter Haining proposed that her model for Dr Frankenstein was Andrew Crosse – and for a very good reason. There is some controversial evidence to suggest that during one of his many mysterious experiments with electricity, performed secretly in his secluded country house at Broomfield, this extraordinary man discovered a means of creating life!

As recorded in his own report of the experiment in question, he had been attempting to create silica crystals by permitting a fluid medium, containing hydrochloric acid and a solution of potassium silicate, to pass through a lump of iron oxide, when:

On the fourteenth day from the commencement of this experiment I observed through a lens a few small whitish excrescences or nipples, projecting from about the middle of the electrified stone. On the eighteenth day these projections enlarged, and struck out seven or eight filaments, each of them longer than the hemisphere on which they grew.

On the twenty-sixth day these appearances assumed the form of a perfect insect, standing erect on a few bristles which formed its tail. Till this period I had no notion that these appearances were other than an incipient mineral formation. On the twenty-eighth day these little creatures moved their legs. I must now say that I was not a little astonished. After a few days they detached themselves from the stone, and moved about at pleasure.

In the course of a few weeks about a hundred of them made their appearance on the stone. I examined them with a microscope, and observed that the smaller ones appeared to have only six legs, the larger ones eight. These insects are pronounced to be of the genus acarus, *but*

there appears to be a difference of opinion as to whether they are a known species; some assert that they are not.

I have never ventured an opinion on the cause of their birth, and for a very good reason – I was unable to form one. The simplest solution of the problem which occurred to me was that they arose from ova deposited by insects

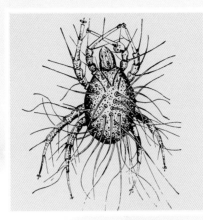

A drawing of one of Crosse's acari.

floating in the atmosphere and hatched by electric action. Still I could not imagine that an ovum could shoot out filaments, or that these filaments could become bristles, and moreover I could not detect, on the closest examination, the remains of a shell ...

I next imagined, as others have done, that they might originate from the water, and consequently made a close examination of numbers of vessels filled with the same fluid: in none of these could I perceive a trace of an insect, nor could I see any in any other part of the room.

If these creatures were indeed acari (i.e. mites), then they were arachnids, not insects, but far more important than their taxonomy is their apparent origin – spontaneously generated from non-living matter, in a solution typically much too caustic to sustain any form of life.

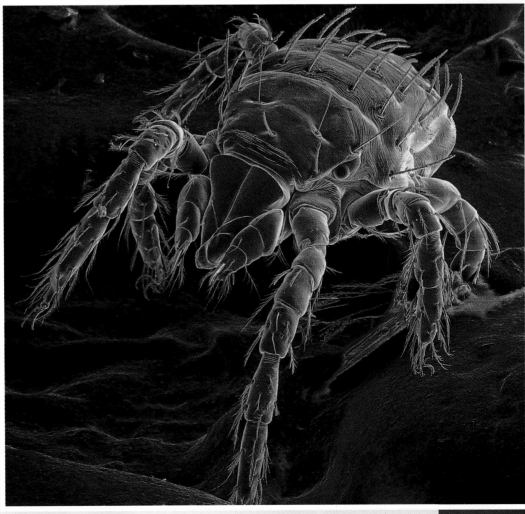

A coloured scanning electron micrograph (SEM) of the Chigger mite (TROMBICULA ALFREDDUGESI), also known as the American harvest mite. Magnification: x 225.

Far from receiving the scientific acclaim that he might have expected from such a sensational result, however, Crosse was subjected to such vitriolic tirades from his peers that he chose to retire from public life, shunned by – and shunning – the world. Yet when fellow electrical researcher W. H. Weeks repeated Crosse's experiments, carefully ensuring that all possible external sources of acari had been excluded from his apparatus, he too succeeded in producing living acari. Even eminent physicist Sir Michael Faraday revealed that he had obtained similar results with some of his own experiments. In 1909, Charles E. Benham urged scientists to repeat Crosse's work to solve this mystery once and for all, but his plea was not heeded. More than 80 years later, the riddle of Crosse's acari remains unexplained.

Perhaps Crosse was just a careless worker who had failed to isolate his apparatus's contents from external contamination. But what if he really did discover the miraculous secret of creating life from the inanimate? A fraud or a Frankenstein – who can say?

IRELAND'S
MOVING STATUES

On 14 February 1985, some of the children in a group of 30 who were praying at St Mary's church in Asdee, County Kerry, claimed to have seen the right hand of a statue of Jesus beckoning them and the eyes of a Madonna statue moving. A month later, some children alleged that a statue in their church at Ballydesmond in County Cork had been moving.

Thus began an extraordinary year in which religious icons all over Ireland reputedly exhibited varying degrees of unexpected mobility. The site of the greatest fervour, however, was the shrine at Ballinspittle, County Cork, whose 152 kg (3 hundredweight) statue of the Virgin Mary was claimed by 17-year-old Clare O'Mahoney and her mother to have rocked backwards and forwards as they walked by its grotto on the evening of 22 July. This initiated a flurry of

The statue of the Virgin Mary at Ballinspittle that was reputedly seen to move.

interest, which led to great numbers of people visiting the shrine during the next four months and numerous allegations that the statue was indeed rocking on its heels, sometimes moving its head and shoulders too. Two days after the O'Mahoneys' sighting, it was watched with some alarm by Sergeant John Murray of the Garda Siochana, who stated that it was vibrating from side to side to such an extent that he had wondered if it was going to fall over.

Happily it did not, but events at Ballinspittle nonetheless reached a dramatically violent climax when, during the early evening of 31 October, two men attacked the Madonna with a hammer and an axe, badly damaging its head,

hands and the illuminated halo around its head. After jeering the horrified crowd for being "stupid fools, worshipping a plaster statue", the two men and a colleague who had been photographing their vandalism jumped in their car and drove off. Although soon caught, they were acquitted at their trial on a legal technicality.

In *The Moving Statue of Ballinspittle*, Lionel Beer listed 47 locations in Ireland that experienced reports of moving statues or other phenomena connected with the Virgin Mary during 1985, and a collection of journalistic accounts concerning these remarkable incidents featured in *Seeing Is Believing: Moving Statues in Ireland*, edited by Colm Toibin.

If they did not comprise authentic miracles, the sightings were presumably due to various optical effects. Investigators of the Asdee reports have shown that an illusion of movement can be effected with the two tall statues in St Mary's church merely by staring for a short time at the small round window between the statues and then gazing at either one of them.

Similarly, the glare of lights illuminating various statues in dark conditions might well have stimulated unconscious eye movements in the observers, thereby eliciting illusory movement by the statues. This is a likely explanation for the many claimed sightings that occurred outdoors at night, or inside churches with subdued lighting.

Another illusion is the autokinetic effect, often experienced by mountaineers, in which stationary objects seen at a distance and lacking a detailed background can appear to move. Perhaps this, coupled with the power of suggestion, always a potent force, was responsible for some reports too. After all, the Ballinspittle Madonna stands over 6 metres (20 feet) away from the viewing area, in a dark alcove on a hillside, from where it would surely be difficult for even the keenest-eyed observers to state categorically that they had detected genuine movement.

Last, but certainly not least, while stopping short of citing mass hallucination, it is evident that if there is a sufficient desire to see something, people will see it, whether it is real or not – a psychological situation arising time and time again with mysterious phenomena.

✦

CROP CIRCLES

Few mysteries have gained such a high public profile so rapidly as the occurrence of crop circles. Prior to 1980, these baffling but beautiful geometrical anomalies that mysteriously appear, usually at night, in fields of corn or other crops were known only to a few farmers. Today they are one of the most famous and visually recognizable enigmas of all

time. Their study even has its own name – cereology.

The variety of crop circles is almost endless, but the simplest form consists of a single circle within which all the corn stems are flattened to the ground but not broken, merely bent over at their base. Often the circle has an outer ring whose stems are also bent, but almost invariably in the opposite direction to those within the remainder of the circle. Sometimes the circle is surrounded by an equidistant series of much smaller circles (satellites), which may or may not be linked to the principal circle by channels. Other circles may contain narrow rings of unbent stems, sandwiched between the main body of the circle and an outermost ring of bent stems.

At first, crop circles seemed to be limited to England's southern counties, but once the phenomenon began to receive media attention, many more examples were reported. Soon, much of Britain was represented by sightings, with reports also coming in from overseas. Explanations offered for their occurrence ranged from rutting hedgehogs or badgers, landing marks left behind by visiting UFOs, and bickering flocks of birds, to fungal infections, over-fertilization and covert military involvement featuring secret weaponry trials.

Not only has the number of sightings increased, so too has the complexity of the circles reported. In their bestseller, *Circular Evidence*, engineers-turned-cereologists Pat Delgado and Colin Andrews suggest that the circles are cryptic pictograms created by some higher cosmic intelligence, and were recognized by the Hopi Indians of Arizona as hieroglyphics disclosing that the world was in grave peril.

A rather more prosaic explanation, but increasingly conceded nowadays by investigators, is that the more intricate the circles become, the less likely it is that they are untouched by human hands, not to mention feet, lawn rollers, and ropes anchored to a central stake. How else can we explain, for instance, the startling occurrence near Royston, Cambridgeshire, in August 1991 of a crop circle exhibiting the perfect configuration of a highly complex computer-generated model from chaos mathematics known as the Mandelbrot

The Mowing Devil, a pamphlet from 1678.

set? There is no question that the hoax factor plays a very prominent part in the occurrence of crop circles, as confirmed by various media exposés and statements from self-confessed fraudsters.

Nevertheless, many of the simpler circles are undoubtedly authentic. After all, some have occurred in remote, inaccessible areas, or in localities rarely visited by anyone, and why waste time producing fake examples here?. The most popular, and to my mind the most plausible, solution to these is the plasma vortex theory, proposed by Dr Terence Meaden, formerly associate professor of physics at Dalhousie University in Canada, more recently editor of the *Journal of Meteorology* and a symposium volume entitled *Circles From the Sky*.

According to Dr Meaden, if a hill obstructs a gust of wind, a vortex is formed, which meets stationary air on the hill's lee side to create a spiralling column that sucks in more air and atmospheric electricity. When this makes contact with the crop field, it spirals, flattening the corn into the familiar configuration of a crop circle. The column's electrical charge also produces the high-pitched noise that has been reported by people just before

Dr Meaden with Gary and Vivienne Tomlinson and the crop circles they saw being formed.

encountering a newly formed circle. Meaden's theory succinctly elucidates not only the physical construction of crop circles but also those rare yet fascinating occasions when eyewitnesses have been fortunate enough to witness the creation of a circle.

One such event occurred in August 1991, when Gary and Vivienne Tomlinson were taking an evening walk in Hambledon, Surrey, at the edge of a cornfield. Suddenly, the corn on their right-hand side began to move. A mist hovered above them and they could hear a strange high-pitched sound. Then a very powerful whirling wind began pushing them from above and all sides, until they could hardly stand upright – except for Gary's hair, responding to the localized build-up of static electricity. Abruptly, the vortex split in two, then raced away, shimmering mistily, and leaving behind two shocked eyewitnesses standing in the middle of a classic crop circle, whose corn stems were flattened all around them.

Further support for Meaden's theory has come from a team of Japanese physicists led by Professor Yoshihiko Ohtsuki, who announced in

June 1991 that they had successfully generated tiny balls of plasma (ionized air) in the laboratory, formed by electromagnetic interference in the air. When these balls made contact with

plates covered in aluminium powder, they created circles and rings corresponding in appearance to crop circles.

Continuing research has also unearthed some very intriguing but hitherto-unrecognized pre-1980 accounts of crop circles. Of particular interest is an illustrated pamphlet from August 1678, in which it is suggested that a "mowing devil" was responsible for an extraordinary configuration in a Hertfordshire oat field that greatly resembles a crop circle. Its present-day significance is indicated by the fact that an 1810 reproduction of this pamphlet was sold to a farmer at a Wiltshire auction in March 1994 for £280.

According to Dr Meaden, however, crop circles may date back considerably further than this. In his book *The Goddess of the Stones*, he boldly speculated that the famous cup and ring decorations favoured by Neolithic artists, ancient mazes, and other vulva-symbolizing geometric designs associated with primeval fertility goddesses may all have been inspired by early man's sightings of crop circles and their energetic creation.

It has often been said that nothing is new in the realms of fashion. The same may also be true, it would seem, in the world of cereology.

Crop formation in the form of the Mandelbrot set near Royston, Cambridgeshire. The formation appeared in August 1991.

GREEN CHILDREN
OF WOOLPIT

The remarkable history of the green children of Woolpit was first documented by two medieval English chroniclers – Ralph, Abbot of Coggeshall, and William of Newburgh. One day during the reign of King Stephen (AD 1135–54), two children were found weeping and wandering, lost and forlorn, in the great pits used to trap wolves at the village of Woolpit, in Suffolk. They caused great amazement among the villagers, but this was due not to their behaviour and their unintelligible dialect but to their appearance – for their clothes, their eyes and, most strikingly, their skin were all green! They were taken to the house of local landowner Sir Richard de Calne, which became their home; but despite all attempts to feed them, for quite a time after their discovery these strange children refused to eat anything other than green beans. Sadly, the younger of the two, a boy, died less than a year later, but the other child, a girl, grew strong and spent the rest of her life in the area.

Over the years, the green tinge to her skin gradually vanished, and when she

The Woolpit church banner.

reached maturity she married a man from King's Lynn in Norfolk. She also learnt English, and was eventually able to inform the villagers that she and the boy had come from a country called St Martin's Land, where there was no sun, only a permanent hazy twilight. They had been following their flocks when they had entered an underground passageway and stumbled out, on the other side, into the bright sunlight of Woolpit.

Many explanations have been offered for this curious story. Because of the children's green skin (the colour of Faerie) and preference for green beans (food of the dead, according to Celtic lore), some researchers have discounted their history as merely a charming folktale. Others have linked it with England's traditional Green Man or Jack-in-the-Green – a leafy supernatural entity personifying fertility and the rebirth of spring. It has even been suggested that the children had originated from a mysterious subterranean world present beneath the surface of the earth and lacking sunlight, or from some parallel dimension through which they had accidentally stepped into our own.

In recent times, a much more literal, sober interpretation has also been put

forward for consideration. During the 1980s, investigator Paul Harris visited Woolpit and learnt that local people generally believe that the story derives from a legend concerning a medieval Norfolk earl who was guardian to two young children. The earl tried unsuccessfully to poison the children with arsenic and then abandoned them in Wayland Wood, in the area of Thetford Forest on the Norfolk–Suffolk border. Here they would surely have died, thus enabling him to take control of the estate that they were due to inherit when they reached adulthood. According to the Woolpit people, these probably became the green children who were later found, still alive but disoriented and ill. Worth noting here is that arsenic poisoning can cause chlorosis, in which the skin turns green. So too can anaemia, a result of malnutrition, from which the abandoned youngsters were likely to have been suffering. A diet-related origin for their green skin would also explain why the girl's complexion reverted to a normal colour once she began to thrive on proper food.

Harris believes that the story's other key portions have straightforward explanations too. For instance, a few miles north-west of Woolpit is a village called Fornham St Martin, which could explain the identity of "St Martin's Land". Further north is Thetford Forest, whose dark interior would certainly seem twilit and sunless to two young children abandoned in its depths. The forest also contains many Neolithic flint mines and associated passages. Perhaps the youngsters wandered into one of them, which led to Woolpit. Furthermore, in the twelfth century most people did not travel very far, so the dialect of children from a distant village may indeed have sounded strange to Woolpit's inhabitants.

There is one final but intriguing twist to the tale of the Woolpit green children. An almost identical story is on record from nineteenth-century Spain, dating from August 1887 and set in the Catalonian village of Banjos. Indeed, apart from the difference in the locality and time, the only notable discrepancy between the two stories is that in the Spanish version the girl dies too, after about five years. Even their liking for

The village sign depicts the Green Children.

The Green Man boss in the cloister ceiling of Norwich Cathedral.

beans is mentioned, and to add coincidence to coincidence, the nobleman who cares for them after their discovery is named as Señor Ricardo da Calno – not exactly dissimilar from Sir Richard de Calne!

This story has been unquestioningly recycled in several books; in *The Monster Trap and Other True Mysteries*, Peter Haining repeated a claim made by John Macklin that the documents and statements of the people who saw and looked after the two green children still exist. In 1986, however, Frank Preston revealed that he had written to the British Council Institute in Barcelona regarding this story, but although the institute conducted extensive searches on his behalf, which included contacting Spanish librarians, museums and town hall archives, as well as searching newspapers from August 1887 for relevant accounts, no trace of the story could be found. This is not surprising, because the village of Banjos does not exist. It is imaginary, just like its green children, whose story is clearly a hoax

devised by someone inspired by the Woolpit version to create a more modern counterpart.

SECRETS OF STONEHENGE

The British Isles are plentifully supplied with standing stones, stone circles and other ancient megaliths: Avebury Henge in Wiltshire, the Rollright Stones in Oxfordshire, Long Meg and Her Daughters in Cumbria, Callanish on Lewis in the Western Isles, the Longstone, one of several standing stones on Dartmoor, and the Ring of Brodgar in Orkney are just a few. None, however, is more famous, or more mysterious, than Stonehenge, standing aloof on Salisbury Plain.

Stonehenge consists of two circles, the outer one composed of sarsen stone (sandstone) pillars formerly supporting

lintels (only six remain), the inner one of bluestones. Inside the latter circle are two series of standing stones, each in the shape of a horseshoe. Once again, the outer series is of sarsen stones, the inner of bluestones. None of the circles or horseshoes is complete. Some of the stones have fallen, others are missing altogether. Inside the innermost horseshoe is a single stone, broken in half, called the Altar Stone, and surrounding the outermost circle is a ring of 56 holes called the Aubrey Holes. Intersecting these some 80 yards from the Altar Stone is the Heel Stone.

The sarsen stones are of local origin, but the bluestones are generally believed to have been transported somehow from the Prescelly Mountains in the far south-west of Wales. According to more radical ideas, intermingled with legend, they were brought to Wiltshire from Ireland, via the magical powers of the magician Merlin, and to Ireland from Africa, by giants!

It is popularly but erroneously believed that Stonehenge was constructed by the druids. In fact, Stonehenge was first constructed around 4000 years ago, during the Neolithic "New Stone" Age. It has been modified several times since then, most recently around 1400 BC, during the Early Bronze Age, producing the version that exists in incomplete form today.

This much is fairly clear, but far less certain is the precise function of this awe-inspiring edifice. Just what was Stonehenge – solar temple, lunar observatory, source of healing energy, extraterrestrial monument? Numerous theories, from the arcane to the absurd, have been proposed. A great deal has been written about the supposed alignments of certain of its stones with celestial events, leading to the conclusion that Stonehenge was created as a complex astronomical observatory; and it is true, for instance, that the line between the Heel Stone and the Altar Stone extends to the precise point of midsummer sunrise. More recently, however, as pointed out by Janet and Colin Bord in *Ancient Mysteries of Britain*, researches have exposed flaws in some of these alignments, thus necessitating a re-examination of the role of Stonehenge in this capacity.

Stonehenge – 4000 years old, its purpose is still a mystery.

A very different theory about Stonehenge owes its origin to folklore, which claims that, just like those of many other megaliths, its stones have healing properties. This belief was first documented as far back as the twelfth century AD, in Geoffrey of Monmouth's *History of the Kings of Britain*. Moreover, during the "Dragon Project" research programme initiated in 1978 by earth energy investigator Paul Devereux, it was demonstrated that at least one of the Rollright standing stones in Oxfordshire exhibited rapid fluctuations of magnetic energy and a high magnetic field. What is so interesting about this is that for centuries local people with broken or fractured limbs have visited the Rollright Stones in the belief that the stones will mend them – and modern hospital therapy has revealed that electromagnetism does accelerate the healing process of bone fractures. Is this just a coincidence?

Perhaps such forces were known to the builders of Stonehenge and other megalithic structures, who erected them in sites that could tap into the earth's natural energy sources for this purpose. Again, the "Dragon Project" has shown that many megaliths are situated on or near to geological faults, associated tectonic intrusions or areas releasing radiation.

Considerations of earth energy lead inevitably to the subject of ley lines – straight lines linking prehistoric or pre-Christian monuments, sacred sites and ancient magical localities, and which may visually delineate a vast network of underground channels of earth energy. Although such ideas were first seriously applied to the British Isles as recently as 1921, by amateur investigator Alfred Watkins, in China the reality of lung mei or "dragon paths" (inspiring the name for Devereux's project) has been accepted for countless centuries. Not only that, it

provides an intriguing parallel with the concept of energy meridians fundamental to the practice of acupuncture, another ancient Chinese tradition.

In the West, the subject of earth energy still incites controversy, but many no longer doubt its existence, or its power. One forceful demonstration of the latter was experienced by a very startled youth called William Lincoln on the evening of 25 August 1974. He and three friends had just entered a ring of beech trees encompassing an ancient earthwork circle called Chanctonbury Ring, an intersection of five leys on a hilltop at Washington, West Sussex, when he was suddenly raised more than a metre into the air by an invisible force. Here he remained for at least 30 seconds, suspended horizontally and screaming with fear, before falling down to the ground – a stark reminder, perhaps, of the potency of the past even in the present day?

A Gathering of Ghosts

BRITAIN'S GHOSTLY ROYAL FAMILY

Many of Britain's most famous cyclical (imprint) ghosts are of former monarchs or consorts who seem unwilling, or unable, to relinquish the present for the past. A cyclical apparition is a recurring phenomenon, triggered by certain environmental conditions. At least four are said to haunt various parts of Windsor Castle – Henry VIII in the deanery, Elizabeth I in the library, Charles I in the Canon's House, and George III in the room where he was restricted during his periods of madness. Sightings of George III have also been reported from Kensington Palace, where the spectre of his predecessor, George II, who died here, is sometimes seen gazing at the weather vane. Hampton Court is home to the spirits of three of Henry VIII's six wives – Anne Boleyn, Jane Seymour, who carries a lighted taper as she walks from the Queen's Apartments, and Catherine Howard, giving voice to terror-stricken shrieks.

Anne Boleyn's ghost is either fond of travelling or has a number of replicates because she has been reported elsewhere too. A brightly illuminated, gliding version has been spied on Tower Hill, she was imprisoned in the Tower of London before her execution. Each year on the anniversary of her execution (19 May), she appears at Blickling Hall in Norfolk where she lived for a time as a child, but her arrival foretells her ultimate doom, for she is headless, her head in her lap, inside a coach drawn by four headless horses.

The Tower of London was a prison to other noble personages down through

Anne Boleyn, second wife of Henry VIII

the centuries, and this is reflected in the assortment of apparitions reported there, including Henry VI, the two Princes in the Tower (Edward V and his brother) and Lady Jane Grey. A very different grey lady, believed to be the ghost of Mary I, who overthrew Lady

Jane, frequents the tapestry room of Sawston Hall in Cambridgeshire; and Mary's mother, Catherine of Aragon, lives on in Kimbolton Castle, Huntingdon, where she died in 1536.

A more recent member of Britain's ghostly royal family is George IV, who acted as Prince Regent during George III's periods of insanity. He is sometimes seen walking along one or other of two underground passages linking the Brighton Pavilion and the Dome concert hall, which was a stable when he was alive. At the other end of the royal time scale is William II, killed while hunting in the New Forest in 1100, but still seen today on the Cadnam to Romsey road, the route taken by the cart carrying his dead body all those years ago.

Perhaps the most astonishing, and distant, member of Britain's royalty to linger in a contemporary limbo of the lost, however, is none other than Boadicea (Boudicca), Queen of the Iceni, who committed suicide during the first century AD rather than be captured by the Romans. The many centuries that have passed since then have created a Britain immeasurably different from the one she knew, but she has still not abandoned it, for a spectacular apparition of this valiant warrior queen riding her chariot has occasionally been sighted even in modern times, emerging from mist near Ermine Street, a Roman road in Lincolnshire.

TERRIFYING TRANSPORT

Not all ghosts are human or animal; some of the strangest are of the very animatedly inanimate variety! One of the most gruesome examples must surely be the death coach of Lady Mary Howard that reputedly haunts the old King's Way moorland road between Tavistock and Okehampton in Devon. Imprisoned inside is the wan spectre of Lady Howard, daughter of a seventeenth-century estate owner called Sir John Fitz of Fitzford, and the coach itself is constructed from the skulls and bones of her four husbands, all of whom were supposedly murdered by her. Even the coach dog running in front of it is a skeleton.

On the evening of 28 June 1944 at around 9.45 p.m., David Hanchet was cycling home and had just reached the junction of Bell Lane in Enfield Old Town, on London's northern outskirts, when he saw a tall black box-shaped coach driven by a coachman and drawn by a team of black horses suddenly drive straight through a hedge bordering some allotments to his left. Totally silent but outlined by an electrical blue light, the coach ran parallel with the hedge for a while, with its wheels about a foot above the ground, then disappeared through the gates of an old garage. The coachman was wearing a tall black hat, a long whip was at his side, and several people were inside. A young boy riding a bike nearby also saw this extraordinary apparition and fled in terror. This is just one of many sightings of an eerie spectral coach running along Bell Lane, and according to legend it is the coach of King James II's notorious "hanging judge", George Jeffreys, who rides inside.

A much more modern mode of phantom transport was reported by many people during 1936 – nothing less, in fact, than a ghostly No. 7 double-decker bus! Bright red in colour, it raced down St Mark's Road, Kensington, on several occasions in the middle of the night, brightly lit inside and with headlights blazing, but no passengers or crew could be seen. A number of car drivers coming along this road swerved in panic to avoid it, but the novelty of a supernatural double-decker swiftly vanished when one driver, unnerved by this frightening apparition, crashed into a wall and was killed. Soon afterwards the wall was demolished and the road widened to make the area safer – and the phantom bus was never seen again.

Also on file are recent reports of a ghostly Spitfire seen and heard near Biggin Hill airfield on London's southern fringes, and a spectral Wellington bomber in Dyfed flying over the Towy valley between Llandeilo and Llandovery, where Wellington bombers trained during the Second World War.

Most eerie of all, however, must surely be phantom road accidents, in which the transport is real but the victim a ghost. Driving along the A12 towards Great Yarmouth on the rainy evening of 2 November 1981, Andrew Cutajar was near to Hopton when he saw a grey mist in the middle of the road. As he drew nearer, it resolved itself into the form of a tall long-haired man dressed in a long coat or cloak and wearing old-fashioned lace-up boots. The figure made no attempt to move out of the way, so Cutajar braked to avoid him, but as he did so his car skidded on the wet road and plunged straight into the man – and out the other side! The man was no more substantial than a cloud and just vanished. Cutajar's car crashed into the grass verge, but happily he was uninjured. As for his "victim", it turns out that this is just one of several similar incidents reported from this stretch of road, seemingly haunted by the ghost of a man from an earlier century with no knowledge of modern traffic!

SPRING-HEELED JACK

For a number of years during the nineteenth century, London was terrorized by two veritable fiends in human form known only as Jack, and whose identities remain as much a mystery today as they were then. One was a horrific serial killer – Jack the Ripper. The other was an even more grotesque figure, who may not even have been human – Spring-heeled Jack.

The saga of Spring-heeled Jack appears to have begun in September 1837, when three women and one man, all in separate incidents and all in or near London, were attacked by a weird cloaked figure with pointed ears, talon-like claws, protruding eyes that glowed like blazing orbs and the ability to spit huge flames from his mouth. Equally bizarre was his capability of leaping immense distances through the air, often clearing walls and sometimes even houses in a single enormous leap and thus foiling all attempts made to capture him.

On the evening of 18 February 1838, teenage sisters Margaret and Lucy Scales were walking home through the Limehouse district after visiting their older brother when a tall phantom-like figure holding a small lamp leapt out of the shadows encompassing the entrance to Green Dragon Alley. Without uttering a word, he opened his mouth and spurted great flames of blue fire into Lucy's face, before bounding out of sight moments later as Lucy fell to the floor, gripped by a quivering spasm of fear that lasted for several hours afterwards.

Two nights later in East London, someone rang the bell at the gate of the house where 18-year-old Jane Alsop lived with her parents. When Jane opened the door, she could see a tall thin figure standing in the shadows, wearing an expansive black cloak and some form of helmet. Thinking that he was a policeman, she stepped forward and the man cried out to her to bring him a light quickly, because his colleagues had captured the infamous Spring-heeled Jack. After fetching a candle, she ran outside with it, but when she gave it to the supposed policeman, she received a terrifying shock. As reported by *The Times* two days later:

He threw off his outer garment, and applying the lighted candle to his breast, presented a most hideous and frightful appearance, and vomited forth a quantity of blue and white flame from his mouth, and his eyes resembled red balls of fire … He wore a large helmet, and his dress [tunic], which appeared to fit him very tight, seemed to her to resemble white oil skin.

On the tombstone, with upraised arms and rage in every feature, towered the terrific form of Spring-Heeled Jack. Freezer and Links stood transfixed; their ghastly burden slipped slowly to the grass, but they remained gaping, terror-struck. Vengeance had fallen!

Spring-heeled Jack features on the front cover of a popular 'penny dreadful' (circa late nineteenth century).

foul marshes and suffused with the stink of disease and death. Here, amid abject poverty and squalor, a meagre existence was eked out by the flotsam and jetsam of humanity, among whom was a 13-year-old prostitute called Maria Davis. On that fateful day, while observed by several people close by, Maria was walking along a bridge spanning a particularly vile stretch of marsh called Folly Ditch when Spring-heeled Jack abruptly appeared. Seizing her by the shoulders, he breathed a flurry of flames into her face, then in an almost nonchalant manner he picked up the screaming girl and threw her over the side of the bridge, directly into the marsh below, where her body swiftly sank into its suffocating depths. Before any of the horrified onlookers could do anything, this evil entity had bounded away, as quickly as he had come, leaving the police to dredge the mud and ooze of Folly Ditch in search of Maria's corpse.

Spring-heeled Jack has never been satisfactorily identified. The only contender with any degree of merit was Henry, the Marquis of Waterford, infamous for his sadistic sense of humour. His general build and protuberant eyes corresponded with Jack's, and he is known to have been in the relevant area at the time of several of the attacks. Moreover, once while making one of his famous escapes, Jack's cloak opened and an elaborate crest containing a large gold "W" was revealed. However, whereas Waterford died in 1859, Jack's activities continued

But worse was to come. Almost blinded by the flames belched into her face by this monstrous apparition, Jane staggered back, and her attacker lunged at her with fingers that seemed to her to be made of metal – as sharp as the talons of some great beast or bird of prey, shredding her dress and tearing the flesh on her arms, neck and shoulders.

Screaming with pain and terror, Jane pulled out of his grasp and ran towards the door, but he was quicker and caught her again, raking her skin and pulling out clumps of her hair. Fortunately, her frantic cries alerted her two sisters in the house, who ran outside and freed her.

All three of the women then fled inside and slammed the door, but Jack refused to go away, until in answer to the sisters' frantic cries from an upstairs window some genuine policemen nearby came running. When he saw them, Jack escaped across a field in a series of huge bounds, dropping his cloak in his haste.

So far, his attacks, although terrifying, were not fatal, but all that changed one day in 1845 when Spring-heeled Jack transformed himself from a deranged madman into a callous murderer. At that time, Jacob's Island in Bermondsey was a sleazy slum area containing a number of filthy, decaying houses surrounded by

Jacob's Island, Bermondsey.

for many years afterwards, and as far afield as East Anglia and Everton in Liverpool, scene of his last known appearance, in September 1904.

Equally mystifying are his astounding feats. The common assumption that his immense leaps were achieved using shoes fitted with powerful springs was conclusively (and painfully) disproved when German soldiers wearing such shoes during the Second World War tried to emulate Jack. None succeeded, and almost all of them broke their ankles! Comparing his flame-spitting talent with that of fire-eaters is futile too, because fire-eaters cannot generate fire inside their mouths in the way that Jack did. And how can we explain his razor-sharp metallic talons and his macabre glowing eyes?

Inevitably, some investigators have speculated that Spring-heeled Jack was not human and that he had entered our world from some other dimension or planet. Curiously, a figure very similar in appearance and leaping abilities was observed bounding up into a tree by three people in Houston, Texas, on 18 June 1953. Once in the tree, he simply disappeared and immediately afterwards an unidentified rocket-shaped object was seen and heard rising up through the sky over the rooftops.

Was this a recent visitation from Spring-heeled Jack or another of his kind? If so, let us hope that the twentieth century was less to his liking than the nineteenth, and that he never again returns!

✦ THE BIG GREY MAN OF BEN MACDHUI

With a height of 1309 metres (4296 feet), Ben MacDhui is the loftiest peak in the Cairngorms and the second highest peak anywhere in Scotland. It also has another claim to fame – that of a haunted mountain, because many mountaineers are certain that it harbours a malign humanoid entity, referred to locally as Am Fear Liath Mor, the Big Grey Man.

Ben MacDhui's sinister occupant first came to widespread notice when eminent climber Professor Norman Collie recalled to a stunned audience at the Annual General Meeting of the Cairngorm Club in Aberdeen (December 1925) that in 1891 he had been descending from this mountain's summit through heavy mist when suddenly: "I began to think I heard something else than merely the noise of my own footsteps. For every few steps I took I heard a crunch, and then another crunch as if someone was walking after me but taking steps three or four times the length of my own."

At first Collie tried to make light of such fancies, but the sound persisted, though its agent remained hidden in the mist. As he continued walking "... and the eerie crunch, crunch, sounded behind me, I was seized with terror and took to my heels, staggering blindly among the boulders for four or five miles". Vowing never to return there alone, he remained convinced that there was "something very queer about the top of Ben MacDhui".

This chilling account, coupled with the unquestionable reliability of Collie himself, attracted great media attention. Moreover, other mountaineers began to confess that they too had experienced similar sensations of uncontrollable yet inexplicable fear and panic while on Ben MacDhui (some had scarcely avoided plummeting over the edge of its cliffs in their terror and overwhelming compulsion to leave as quickly as possible) and had come away with the

vivid impression that a malevolent, paranormal presence existed here, which sought to frighten away anyone venturing upon this lonely, desolate peak. There have even been sightings of a huge, man-like figure, strains of ghostly music and laughter have been heard wafting across its shadowy slopes, and many accounts of heavy footsteps like those heard by Collie have been documented.

Reports are not wholly confined to Ben MacDhui either. One day during the early 1920s, while coming down alone from Braeraich in Glen Eanaich, which is close to Ben MacDhui, experienced mountaineer Tom Crowley heard footsteps behind him. When he looked around, he was horrified to see a huge grey mist-shrouded figure with pointed ears, long legs and finger-like talons on its feet. He did not stay for a closer look.

Wales's answer to the Big Grey Man is the Grey King, also known as the Brenin Llwyd or Monarch of the Mist. Said to frequent Snowdon, Cader Idris, Plynlimon, and other lofty peaks, this awesome entity was greatly feared in times past as a child-stealer, and even the mountain guides were nervous of venturing into its domain.

Explanations offered for the Big Grey Man are very diverse. They range from a yeti-like man-beast, a mystical holy man, a geological holograph, and an optical illusion comparable to the famous Brocken spectre, to a marooned extraterrestrial, a visitor-induced energy trace image, an electromagnetic

Ben MacDui looks tranquil enough, but does it harbour a sinister presence?

phantom, and a hallucination engendered by oxygen deficiency.

There is also another noteworthy possibility. In view of the vast variety of unexplained phenomena reported from Ben MacDhui over the years, could this mountain be a "window" area – an interface between different dimensions or alternate worlds? If so, there is a good chance that such a significant portal would have a guardian, to deter would-be intruders or trespassers. Is it just coincidence that this is the precise effect so successfully accomplished by Ben MacDhui's mysterious Big Grey Man?

SCREAMING SKULLS, WAILING BANSHEES ... AND A TALKING MONGOOSE

Many ghostly phenomena are predominantly visual, but Britain can boast some emphatically audible examples too. One of the most macabre is the screaming skull of Bettiscombe Manor, Dorset. Several different versions of its history have been documented, but according to the most familiar one it is the skull of a West Indian black slave, whose master, John Frederick Pinney of Bettiscombe Manor, promised to send his body to his homeland for burial when he died. Sadly, however, Pinney broke his promise, burying him in Bettiscombe churchyard instead. Every night from then on, the churchyard and manor echoed with the sounds of terrible screams and groans, until the corpse of Pinney's slave was disinterred and brought into the manor. The sounds stopped, but at some time in the future the corpse mysteriously vanished, except for its yellowing skull. Since then, according to local lore, the skull has been taken out of the manor on several occasions – and each time the area has been plagued by devastations, including livestock deaths,

THE CORNISH OWLMAN

During 1976, several children and teenage girls independently spied a strange feathered "owlman" near the church at Mawnan, a small village on the south coast of Cornwall. Judging from the sketch made by eyewitness June Melling, 12, who saw it hovering over the church tower on 17 April, it resembled a man with feathered wings, pointed ears and a black beak. By contrast, it appears much more owl-like in a drawing prepared by Sally Chapman, one of two teenage girls who reportedly observed this entity on 3 July, as it stood amid some pine trees in the woods near the church and then took flight. According to Sally and fellow eyewitness Barbara Perry, it was like a big owl the size of a man, with glowing red eyes, pointed ears and pincer-like feet. Sally's description and sketch recall the European eagle owl *Bubo bubo*, an extremely large species not native to Britain but a frequent escapee from collections, with bright orange eyes, prominent ear tufts and huge talons on its feet. Further sightings occurred near Mawnan church in 1978, after which it seemed to vanish from existence.

During the late 1980s, however, a teenager whom I shall identify only as Gavin (now an undergraduate zoology student) was walking with his girlfriend one summer evening through woodlands in the vicinity of Mawnan when they saw the owlman standing on a thick branch in a large conifer tree, with its wings raised. Grey and brown in colour, with glowing eyes, it seemed around 1.25 metres (4 feet) tall, and they discerned two huge toes on the front of each foot. When the creature saw its eyewitnesses, "...its head jerked down and forwards, its wings lifted and it just jumped backwards. As it did its legs folded up." Its behaviour once again calls to mind a very large owl, although Gavin is not sure what it was. Some researchers deem the owlman to be a zooform entity, or simply a hoax. The simple truth is that we just don't know.

Birdman monster. Seen on 3rd July, quite late at night but not quite dark. Red eyes. Black mouth. It was very big with great big wings and black claws. Feathers grey.
B. Perry 4th July 1976.

I saw this monster bird last night. It stood like a man then it flew up through the trees. It is as big as a man. Its eyes are red and shine brightly.
Sally Chapman 4/7/76.

F. Marion Crawford's classic ghost story **The Screaming Skull** illustrated by L. Ward in a 1936 edition.

· I·SAW·THE·BANSHEE·FLYING· ·
· WILD·IN·THE·WIND·OF·MARCH ·

A banshee, illustrated by Florence Harrison (circa 1910).

from an Irish family who emigrated to the USA in 1848, allegedly heard the banshee's fearful shriek just after noon. Later that day, O'Barry learnt that one of his friends had been assassinated: his friend was President John F. Kennedy.

A Welsh equivalent to the banshee is a disembodied moaning cry known as the cyhyraeth or death sound, which haunts a number of old Welsh families. It has recently been reported in the region of the River Towy. Another audible augury of doom is a drum that once belonged to Sir Francis Drake. Now housed at Buckland Abbey, once Drake's home, it is said to beat of its own accord at times of national crisis. Events at which the drum has supposedly sounded include the surrender of the German fleet in Scapa Flow in the Orkney Islands in 1918, and the retreat from Dunkirk in June 1940.

Perhaps the most bizarre vocal apparition documented in Britain was a talking mongoose called Gef, which purportedly haunted the Irving family's isolated farmhouse, Doarlish Cashen, on the Isle of Man's western coast, during the 1930s. Although many people visited their home and heard Gef, only the Irvings claimed to have seen him clearly. Some investigators believe that Gef was a mischievous poltergeist, whereas others have concluded that the Irvings' teenage daughter, Voirrey, was an accomplished ventriloquist.

exceptionally violent weather that destroyed crops, and unearthly screams, all of which have ceased once the skull has been returned.

A chilling tale, but whether there is any truth to it is quite another matter. When the skull was examined by Professor Gilbert Causey of the Royal College of Surgeons, he stated that it was in fact the skull of a prehistoric woman. If so, it may have come from one of the ancient barrows on the Dorset Downs.

Other screaming skulls have been documented at Burton Agnes Hall in Yorkshire, Wardley Hall in Manchester, Calgarth House beside Lake Windermere, Warbleton Priory Farm in Sussex and Higher Farm at Chilton Cantelo in Somerset.

According to Irish lore, the banshee is a supernatural entity in the form of a weeping woman who haunts certain ancient Irish families (even outside Ireland), and whose terrible wailing cry warns of an impending death within the family or its circle of friends. Perhaps the most dramatic recent case occurred on 22 November 1963, when Boston businessman James O'Barry, descended

DEVIL'S HOOFPRINTS

The Times is not known for carrying unreliable or sensationalized information, which is why the general public and scientific world alike took particular notice of a report that appeared in its 16 February 1855 issue, from which the extract below is drawn:

Considerable sensation has been evoked in the towns of Topsham, Lympstone, Exmouth, Teignmouth, and Dawlish ... It appears that, on Thursday night last [8 February] there was a very heavy fall of snow in the neighbourhood of Exeter and the south of Devon. On the following morning the inhabitants of the above towns were surprised at discovering the footmarks of some strange and mysterious animal, endowed with the power of ubiquity, as the footprints were to be seen in all kinds of unaccountable places – on the tops of houses and narrow walls, in gardens and courtyards, enclosed by high walls and palings, as well as in open fields. There was hardly a garden in Lympstone where these footprints were not observable. The track appeared more like that of a biped than of a quadruped, and the steps were generally eight inches in advance of each other. The impression of the foot closely resembled that of a donkey's shoe, and measured from an inch and a half to (in some instances) two and a half inches across [38–63 mm]. Here and there it appeared as if cloven, but in the generality of the steps the shoe was continuous, and, from the snow in the centre remaining entire, merely showing the outer crest of the foot, it must have been convex.

It was not long before the more superstitious-minded voiced the opinion that these bewildering prints were of diabolical origin, and so they became known as the devil's footprints or hoofprints. This was but one of many explanations proffered, including unusual meteorological effects, or the tracks of otters, rats, herons, wood mice, an escaped kangaroo, swans, cats, dogs, badgers, hares, donkeys, or even a still-

The wood mouse (APODEMUS SYLVATICUS) is extremely agile.

undiscovered species of albatross-like bird making a fleeting visit from its secret polar domain.

The most recent, and certainly the most novel, solution proposed was that of Manfri Frederick Wood in his book *In the Life of a Romany Gypsy*, claiming that according to Romany recollections the tracks were the product of a well-orchestrated exercise featuring seven Romany tribes using more than 400 sets of measure stilts with size 27 boots at their base! The purpose was to scare superstitious Didekais and Pikies from the area.

No known meteorological effect can create these "hoofprints", and all but one of the animal contenders are too large. Moreover, according to certain other reports of that February night's strange event, some tracks passed through drain-pipes and tiny holes in hedges, and even stopped abruptly in the middle of open fields.

The only creature whose tracks are small enough, and can also explain these anomalies, is the wood mouse *Apodemus sylvaticus*. This species is extremely adept at climbing up and over all manner of surfaces and structures. It can also run through drain-pipes and squeeze through minuscule gaps. And a wood mouse scampering across a white, snow-covered field would soon be spotted and snatched off the ground by any owl close by, thus bringing its tracks to a sudden end.

Reviewing this case in 1964, zoologist Alfred Leutscher revealed how the wood mouse's four paws collectively produce a horseshoe-shaped print when hopping through snow, just like those found in Devon, and he recalled seeing in Epping Forest many such tracks made in the snow by wood mice during the severe winter of 1962–63. It was an exceptionally severe winter when the tracks occurred in Devon, so with less food available than normal the area's wood mice may have been unusually bold in searching for nourishment – a plausible scenario that also explains why such tracks have not been seen very often since.

Rat Kings, Tatzelworms and Other Baffling Beasts

✴

RAT KINGS

On 13 July 1748, German miller Johann Heinrich Jager found that his mill at Gross Ballheiser (also spelt "Grossballhausen") contained more than just flour when a bizarre aggregation of 18 living rats fell out from between two stones underneath the cogwheels. Remarkably, the rats were all inextricably linked to one another by their tails, which were intertwined in a knot of gordian proportions. This type of conjoined collection of rats is called a rat king or roi de rats, possibly a corruption of rouet de rats – "rat wheel", and quite a number of examples have been documented in Europe during the past few centuries.

Perhaps the most dramatic case on record featured the discovery by some farm workers in December 1822 of two rat kings together, within a hollow beam in the attic of a barn in the eastern German village of Döllstedt. One of the kings contained 28 rats, the other had 14. Yet even these do not compare to the monstrous example found desiccated and hairless in a miller's chimney at Buchheim, Germany, in May 1828. Its rats, probably not adults, comprised an amazing 32 individuals in total. This emperor among kings was duly preserved for posterity and is now a prized possession of the Altenberg Mauritianum.

In *Rats*, Martin Hart devoted a chapter to rat kings and listed 56 different examples, 38 of which he considered to be authentic (some fake rat kings have been deliberately manufactured over the years to sell at high prices to unwary curio collectors).

A rat ring or roi de rats – the result of a bizarre intertwining of the creatures' tails.

All but one feature the black rat *Rattus rattus*; the exception is a king of 10 young field rats *R. brevicaudatus*, found in Bogor, Java, on 23 March 1918. A king of young wood mice *Apodemus sylvaticus* was discovered in April 1929 at Holstein, and there are a few squirrel kings on record too. The most recent rat king seems to be a seven-specimen example found by Dutch farmer P. van Nijnatten in his barn at Rucphen, North Brabant, in February 1963.

How can rat kings be explained? Some French investigators have proposed that the linking of specimens may occur before the birth of a litter, so that the litter's rats are born as a king. If so, this would be similar to the little-known phenomenon of cat kings – litters of kittens born with grossly intertwined umbilical cords. As some of the largest rat kings have contained adults, however, a prenatal origin cannot explain all, if any, such kings. After all, as the members of a king are unlikely to be able to obtain much food, they surely could not survive from birth to maturity in an inseparably linked condition.

Alternatively, if a group of rats find themselves in a confined damp space, they may huddle close to one another, pressing and wrapping their tails together, so that the tails adhere in a knotted mass. In a bid to uncover the kings' secret, the Rucphen specimen was X-rayed, which revealed that the tails were indeed knotted, resulting in some tail fractures and signs of a callus formation. These indicated that the knot had occurred quite some time in the past, but just how the knot had formed remains a mystery.

THE ALPINE TATZELWORM

One day during the summer of 1921, a poacher and a herdsman were hunting on Hochfilzenalm mountain in southern Austria when they saw a bizarre animal watching them. Resting on a rock, it resembled a grey worm, 60–90 cm (2–3 feet) long and as thick as a man's arm. The poacher decided to shoot the creature and pointed his rifle at it, but just as he did so it leapt at the men, performing a considerable aerial arc and revealing that it possessed two short front legs. Needless to say, the men fled at once, leaving their uncanny adversary far behind.

This is just one of countless reports on file describing a seemingly undiscovered species of reptile or amphibian native to the Swiss, Bavarian and Austrian Alps of Central Europe,

In 1954, Sicilian farmers reported seeing a cat-like creature with a serpent's body.

and referred to by the local inhabitants of this alpine terrain as the tatzelworm (clawed worm) or stollenworm (hole-dwelling worm). Judging from a report from farmers describing a strange cat-headed serpentine beast with only two front limbs that was seen attacking a herd of pigs near Palermo, Sicily, in 1954, creatures resembling the tatzelworm might also exist in parts of southern Europe.

Science may have narrowly missed the chance of uncovering the tatzelworm's identity in 1924, for this was when two travellers in the Mur Valley discovered what seemed to be the partial skeleton of a 120-cm- (4-foot) long lizard. It was looked at by a veterinary student, who suggested that it comprised the remains of a roe deer carcase, though this was disputed by its finders because of discrepancies between its features and those of deer. Unfortunately the skeleton was afterwards discarded without anyone else examining it. Interestingly, just two years later a creature said to resemble a giant lizard was encountered by a 12-year-old shepherd boy at precisely the same spot where the controversial skeleton had been found. The boy was so terrified by the experience that he refused to tend sheep there for the rest of that summer.

The description given by the poacher and herdsman in 1921 fits that of most tatzelworms on record, with one notable exception. Different eyewitnesses have given different limb counts. Some claim that this species has only a single, front pair of legs; others say that it has two pairs of legs; a few say that it has no legs at all. In general appearance it is likened to a worm-like lizard or salamander. None of these identities is impossible. There is a group of widely distributed lizards called skinks, some of which have two pairs of small limbs, others just a single tiny front pair. Similarly, while most salamanders have two small pairs, the North American sirens have only a front pair.

Some zoologists have favoured a relationship between the tatzelworm and the American Gila monster *Heloderma suspectum*, a species of poisonous lizard, or with the glass snake *Ophisaurus apodus*, a large legless lizard from southern Europe.

THE MARK OF THE WEREWOLF

Before scientific advances began to sweep aside the Dark Ages' all-embracing shadows of superstition, ignorance and religious fanaticism, much of Europe's population lived in very real fear of werewolves – humans who could transform themselves into wolves. In those days people had great faith in the reputed power of the plant wolfsbane (monkshood) to ward off these evil shapeshifters. Another practice was to shoot suspected individuals with blessed silver bullets.

Traditional measures for determining whether a person was a werewolf involved looking out for signs that were as vague as they were numerous. Suspicion could fall upon anyone with any of the following traits: protruding teeth, hairy hands or feet, ears that were pointed and small or positioned low and towards the back of the head, unusually long third fingers, thick eyebrows joining on the bridge of the nose, and long curved fingernails tinged with red. People eating the brains or roasted flesh of a wolf, or the meat from a sheep killed by a wolf, were certain to become werewolves; this was also the dire fate awaiting those who drank from puddles forming in wolf footprints or at water-holes frequented by wolves.

All in all, it is surprising that anyone escaped suspicion and it certainly explains the extraordinary abundance of werewolf trials during the Middle Ages. France, for instance, staged an incredible 30,000 trials just between the years 1520 and 1630, as confirmed in public records still existing from that period.

One of the most famous of these trials featured a recluse called Gilles Garnier. During the summer of 1573, the partially devoured corpses of several slaughtered children were found in the area of Dôle, and a number of local peasants claimed to have spied a strange wolf-like beast with Garnier's face. In November of that year a group of villagers, following the sound of a young girl's terrified screams, discovered her, still alive but badly wounded, in the clutches of a huge wolf fitting this description. Although the wolf escaped, Garnier was arrested a few days later, together with his wife. At the trial, Garnier freely confessed to two of the killings attributed to this creature, and even stated that he had taken home a portion from the body of one of his victims, which was duly eaten by his wife. Not surprisingly, both defendants were found guilty and were burned alive in January 1574.

Bearing in mind that the direct physical transformation of a human into a wolf –or any other creature – is a fundamental biological impossibility, it seems far more likely that Garnier was simply insane. Indeed, he may not even have committed the crimes: recluses lacking friends or influence have always been popular as scapegoats for the evil deeds of others.

Some werewolf trials adopted a more enlightened attitude, as with Jacques Rollet from Caude in western France, who had murdered and eaten several people before he was captured in 1598 while dismembering yet another victim. After hearing his claim that he could transform himself into a wolf and seeing that he was clearly mentally subnormal, the judge committed him to a lunatic asylum. A similar case featured Jean Grenier, a mentally retarded teenage shepherd from the Bordeaux region, who bragged that while in the guise of a wolf he had killed and devoured more than 50 children. Following his trial in 1604, Grenier was given into the care of a local Franciscan monastery where he spent the rest of his life.

Rollet, Grenier, possibly Garnier too, and many other so-called werewolves were undoubtedly suffering from a bizarre but long-recognized mental condition called lycanthropy in which sufferers fervently believe that they can actually turn into a wolf at will. They also behave like wolves, howling at the moon and attacking people using their teeth and nails. Even today, cases of this grotesque, pitiful delusion are occasionally reported from Europe.

Nevertheless, some people in medieval times may have believed that they were turning into wolves not because of lycanthropy but because they had taken various hallucinogenic substances. Some, derived from such plants as henbane and deadly nightshade, are well known for inducing illusions and were widely used for witchcraft purposes. In addition, a grain-contaminating fungus called ergot secretes a compound similar to LSD that causes hallucinatory sensations of shape-shifting. This is very relevant to the prevalence of medieval werewolf claims, because during that period uncontaminated grain was reserved for the aristocracy; peasants wishing to make bread had to use grain contaminated with ergot. Little wonder, then, that some were convinced that they could change themselves into wolves.

Rabid wolves foaming at the mouth, or somebody unfortunate enough to have been bitten by one and thus displaying the same symptoms, are also likely to have been mistaken for werewolves. It is certainly the case that two further supposed traits of werewolves are their frothing mouths and their ability to turn anyone they bite into a werewolf.

In 1990, Hugh Trotti offered what may well be yet another, quite fascinating insight into the werewolf myth. An ancient Egyptian god of death was the jackal-headed deity Anubis, worshipped by a cult whose priests wore a wolf-like mask representing him. This cult eventually transferred to Rome and by the first century AD statues of a jackal-headed human figure called Hermanubis were numerous there. Germanic troops recruited into the Roman armies would have observed priests of Hermanubis wearing their wolf-like masks and seen the jackal-headed statues and would undoubtedly have remembered and spoken of them after the Roman Empire's fall. In turn, as suggested by Trotti, distorted accounts of these could eventually have inspired legends of humans who were able to assume the form of wolves.

✪

GROW YOUR OWN HOMUNCULI

Even today, the alchemists of medieval times remain famous for their supposed, though unconfirmed, ability to transmute base metals into gold, using the fabled philosopher's stone. Less well-remembered, yet even more controversial, is their alleged artificial creation of tiny living humanoids, known as homunculi. Recently, however, Paul Thompson published an engrossing review of this largely forgotten arcane subject in *Fate* (September 1994), which contains some remarkable revelations.

Alchemists claimed that the culture medium required for the growth of homunculi contained several biological fluids such as sputum or egg-white, and sometimes inorganic fluids like dew; but the two substances most commonly cited as essential were human blood and semen, both of which are widely believed in primitive or non-scientific societies to harbour the vital essence of life. Also required was horse manure, whose heat-releasing properties were utilized to incubate the medium.

Bearing in mind that all of the above ingredients are readily obtainable, why was the production of homunculi a skill restricted to alchemists? The answer is

Theophrastus Paracelsus.

that the recipes always seemed to contain one vital ingredient that was exceptionally complex and difficult to prepare. For example, in the homunculus recipe contained within the treatise *De Natura Rerum*, written by the sixteenth-century Swiss scholar Theophrastus Paracelsus, "the arcanum of human blood" was included: essential but esoteric, its constituents were known only to the alchemical fraternity.

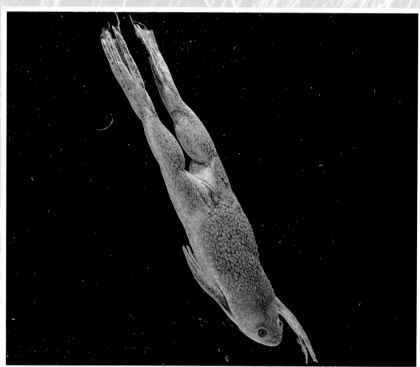

*The African clawed toad (*XENOPUS LAEVIS*) diving through water.*

Equally obscure is "animal tincture", listed in another medieval recipe.

Despite such difficulties, records detailing the successful production of homunculi do exist. An extraordinary specimen grown from distilled human blood and able to emit beams of red light was reputedly cultured and exhibited at the court of King Louis XIV of France by royal physician Dr Borel. The most outstanding case, however, fully documented in Dr Emil Besetzny's book *Sphinx*, must surely be the creation of ten living homunculi in a mere five weeks, accomplished by two Austrian alchemists of the late sixteenth century – Count Johann Ferdinand von Kufstein and Abbé Geloni.

Like all homunculi, they were grown in sealed jars – homunculi die if exposed for any considerable period to the air – filled with water and eventually buried under heaps of manure. They were treated, as usual, with some special, but unspecified, solution, which doubled the size of eight of the homunculi, producing a series of 30-cm- (1-foot) tall specimens.

No two homunculi looked the same and to each was fixed an identity. Eight were physical manikins, known respectively as the king, queen, knight, monk, nun, seraph, miner and architect, and clothes pertinent to their identities were manufactured for them. Each of these eight homunculi was fed with special pink tablets every three to four days and their water was changed once a week. On at least one occasion, the "king" homunculus escaped from his jar, and was earnestly trying to remove the seal on the jar housing the "queen" when he was spotted by Count Kufstein's butler. Chased by Kufstein and the butler, the "king" soon fainted from exposure to the air and was put back inside his own receptacle.

The remaining two homunculi were non-corporeal and only appeared when Geloni tapped their jars and chanted certain magical words. A face would then materialize in each of them; moreover, in one the liquid would turn blue, in the other it would turn red. The red "spirit" homunculus was fed on blood and its water was changed every two to three days, but the blue "spirit" homunculus was never fed and its water was never changed.

All ten homunculi would answer questions concerning future events, invariably predicting correctly the outcomes, and they were observed by many people. These included some very notable personages, like Count Franz Josef von Thun and Count Max Lamberg. Surely, however, such bizarre man-made entities could not really have existed – or could they?

I cannot help but wonder whether these particular homunculi were nothing more than large amphibians brought back by travellers from the tropics. One likely candidate is the African clawed toad *Xenopus laevis*, a common species, vaguely human in shape, which lives permanently in water – perhaps explaining why the "king" fainted soon after escaping from its jar.

No one knows what happened to nine of the homunculi after Geloni and Kufstein ultimately went their separate ways. However, an event occurred that may have left behind some tangible evidence of the tenth. Once, the jar containing the "monk" homunculus was accidentally dropped, smashing as it hit the floor and killing its humanoid inhabitant. His body was afterwards buried in the grounds of Kufstein's Tyrolean residence – but where is this today? If only we knew its locality, the soil around it could be sifted, as suggested by Paul Thompson, and who knows what remains might be found?

One thing is certain: if a 30-cm-long skeleton is ever found under these circumstances, Thompson would be very interested to learn more about it – and so would I.

THE GOLDEN FLEECE – DID IT REALLY EXIST?

One of the most familiar stories in Greek mythology features the quest by the hero Jason and his party of fellow adventurers aboard the *Argo* to obtain the Golden Fleece at Colchis (now part of Georgia). This was the fleece of Chrysomallus, a magical winged ram sent by Hermes to carry away some children from Ino, their evil stepmother. Ino had planned to sacrifice them in the hope of appeasing the gods during a great famine in Boeotia, ancient Greece.

Traditionally, this tale has been dismissed either as total fiction or as a distorted telling of an early search for gold in which an ordinary fleece was used as a sieve to trap gold particles washed down the river Phasis. In 1987, however, Dr G. J. Smith, a researcher in physical chemistry at Melbourne University in Australia, offered up for consideration a radically different theory, which proposed a much more direct, if highly unusual, basis in reality for the allegedly mythical Golden Fleece.

In modern times, farmers often feed their sheep upon leaves during periods of famine. Consequently, Smith suggested that in ancient Greece farmers experiencing such a situation may well have provided their sheep with the leaves of the extensively cultivated olive tree *Olea europaea*. The leaves of this species contain an acid from which chemical compounds known as pentacyclic triterpenoids are derived; sheep that ingest certain of these compounds are known to secrete through their skin's sweatglands a reddish substance called lanaurin, which stains their fleece a distinctive golden colouration.

This has led Smith to speculate that the story of the Golden Fleece may have originated from sightings of sheep that had been fed extensively upon olive tree leaves during the period of severe famine prevalent when this myth apparently arose, and which, therefore, may well have possessed golden, lanaurin-stained wool. It is hardly the most romantic explanation for such a stirring legend, but undeniably thought-provoking.

✪

THE BEAST OF GEVAUDAN

Between June 1764 and June 1767, a considerable number of horrific murders, mostly of women and children, took place in a district of Lozère, in south-eastern France, called Gévaudan. On those few occasions when the assassin was spied, it proved to be a huge wolf-like beast, which dispatched its victims by savagely tearing out their throats before devouring their bodies or simply ripping them apart. To quell the rising tide of panic, in February 1765 King Louis XV sent to Gévaudan a famous hunter called Denneval, accompanied by six highly trained

bloodhounds, but they did not meet with success.

Seven months later, however, it seemed as if the Beast of Gévaudan's bloody reign of terror had finally come to an end, when the king's personal gun-carrier, Antoine de Beauterne, tracked what was assumed to be the creature to a quarry at the bottom of the Bèal Ravine, near the village of Pommier. Here it was shot dead and its immense body, more than 1.5 metres (5 feet) long and weighing 65 kg (143 lb), was transported in triumph to the court of the king. It proved to be a massive black wolf, but it was not the Beast, for the killings continued.

Then on 19 June 1767, another huge wolf was shot, this time at Mount Chauvet by Jean Chastel, after which the killings finally ended. Many people, however, believe that there was more to the history of the Gévaudan Beast than a bloodthirsty, possibly even rabid, wolf. In *La Bête du Gévaudan*, Gérald Ménatory suggested that many of the killings may in fact have been the work of one or more human serial killers, capitalizing upon reports of man-killing wolves to conceal their own murderous attacks.

There is one other theory, even more chilling. Could the Beast of Gévaudan have been a werewolf – performing its gruesome acts as a wolf, and afterwards transforming back into a man to elude discovery? Inevitably, scientists have little time for such an identity. Are we to assume, therefore, that it was just a coincidence that the killings came to an end when Chastel shot the Mount Chauvet wolf ... with a blessed silver bullet?

A woodcut impression of the Beast of Gévaudan, which terrorized Lozère in south-eastern France during the 1760s.

Jason and Medea with the Golden Fleece, in a German engraving.

DENMARK'S GREEN KITTEN

In autumn 1995, Pia Bischoff was surprised to discover a two-month-old kitten outside a hayloft in Dybvad, north-western Denmark. When she took a closer

look at it, however, she was even more surprised – because this curious kitten's fur and claws were bright green! All attempts to wash off its strange hue have been in vain. Vets who have examined the animal and researchers at the university hospital in Copenhagen who have studied samples of its fur claim that it may have been green ever since it was born, noting that the copper patina extends from the tip to the follicle of every hair.

Although this odd colouration could be due to a mutant gene, it seems more likely that the kitten (or even its mother while pregnant) has somehow come into contact with copper-contaminated water. Several years ago, in a town in southern Sweden, water derived from some corroded copper pipes was unmasked as the culprit responsible for the hair of several blonde women turning green!

A satyr portrayed on a fragment of an amphora dating from the sixth century BC.

✴

SEX AND THE SATYRS

In Greek mythology, satyrs were semi-humans with the hairy legs, hooves, tail and short horns of goats; but did they have a basis in reality? This unexpected prospect was raised in a stimulating paper published in the scientific journal *Human Evolution* in 1994 by Dr Helmut Loofs-Wissowa from the Australian National University's Faculty of Asian Studies.

In ancient classical art, satyrs were frequently portrayed with a prominently erect penis, even when engaging in non-sexual activity. Indeed, it was this characteristic that earned them their reputation for sexual licentiousness. However, Dr Loofs-Wissowa believes that this is all fallacious and that in fact the satyrs were displaying a physiological condition known as the penis rectus, in

which the penis assumes a horizontal position even when flaccid. Among modern humans this condition is only recorded from the bushmen of South Africa, but it is often portrayed in prehistoric cave art, including some Upper Palaeolithic examples from Europe, in which the figures exhibiting the penis rectus condition are hairy humanoids.

There are two very intriguing aspects to this. One is that anthropologists have argued that these hirsute figures are representations of Neanderthal man *Homo neanderthalensis*, which is believed to have died out at least 30,000 years ago. The other is that sightings of hairy troll-like humanoids are often reported in many parts of Asia, and these are believed by some scientists to be relict, modern-day Neanderthals, eluding formal scientific discovery. Of particular note here is that eyewitness descriptions of these mystifying entities have often mentioned the odd fact that they seem to have permanently erect penises, apparent even when spied

indulging in non-sexual activity such as eating or walking. This suggests that they are in reality displaying the penis rectus condition.

Combining all this information, Loofs-Wissowa suggests that the penis rectus condition is clearly a marker in human palaeontology, i.e. indicating the identity of Neanderthals. And, as a direct consequence, he boldly proposes that satyrs might actually have been latter-day Neanderthals. He notes that many features attributed to satyrs in artistic representations differentiate them from modern humans but ally them to Neanderthals. These include their hairy body, upturned nose, prominent eye ridges, round head, strong neck and, most noticeable of all, their exhibition of the penis rectus condition, hitherto wrongly identified as an indication that satyrs possessed a hyperactive sex drive.

This is a very novel idea, but it still leaves unexplained the small matter of the satyrs' hooves and tail, not to mention their horns....

VAMPIRES

The vampire myth is a complex concept that has evolved from many different sources. Archaic superstitions, grisly discoveries of premature burials featuring unfortunate sufferers of catalepsy (a form of unconsciousness whose victims appear dead), psychopathic killers with an insane craving for blood, lurid tales of real blood-drinking vampire bats with which the followers of Cortés regaled their aghast public upon their return to Europe from the Americas – these are just a few of its interwoven strands.

The vampire's "evolution" from the early mythological concept of a vitalized corpse to a visibly human entity was greatly assisted by Bram Stoker's novel *Dracula*. His inspiration for the fictional count was a real person from the fifteenth century – Prince Vlad V of Wallachia, now part of Romania, and adjoining the vampires' supposed stronghold, Transylvania. Nicknamed Dracula after his family's emblem, a dragon, "dracul" in the Wallachian tongue, which also means "devil", Prince Vlad was greatly feared for his sadistic bloodlust. His favourite method of dealing with real or imagined foes was to impale their living bodies on stakes, for which he earned another nickname, "Tepes" – the Impaler. He is even believed to have dined upon their flesh and may have drunk their blood too.

There might be more to Vlad Tepes and his vampire connection, however, than murderous insanity. In some allergic reactions to a given substance, sufferers also develop an addiction to that same substance, and if deprived of it they can react in a highly bizarre, deranged manner. In 1985, Idaho physician Dr Thomas McDevitt suggested that the Wallachian tyrant may have suffered from an allergic reaction of this nature in relation to blood, explaining his obsession with blood-letting and the hideous methods that he devised to achieve it. Moreover, portraits of the prince depict him with dark circles beneath his eyes, puffy cheeks and a sallow pallid complexion

– classic characteristics of some types of allergy victim.

Publicly aired in 1982 by Professor David Dolphin from the University of British Columbia in Vancouver, another medically inspired explanation for vampires is that they are suffering from a congenital blood disorder known as iron-deficiency porphyria, subsequently dubbed "the Dracula disease". The metabolism of sufferers is very inefficient in combining iron with complex compounds called porphyrins to yield haem, an intrinsic component of the blood pigment haemoglobin. As a result, their skin becomes increasingly impregnated with iron-free porphyrins, which are stimulated by daylight to incite a chain of reactions causing skin lesions and other disfigurements. To avoid this, sufferers tend to emerge only at night. Further increasing their vampire-like traits, another outcome of this disease is a tightening of the gums, which causes the teeth to protrude.

Bearing in mind that any haem which *is* present in the system of this disease's sufferers is exceedingly valuable, substances that destroy haem and thus remove precious iron from their bodies can be lethal to such

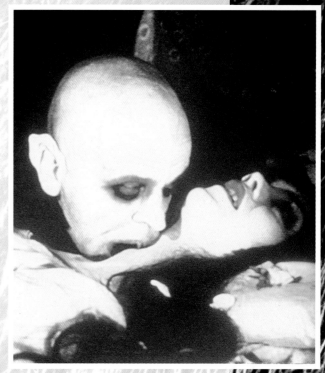

Fount of inspiration: twentieth-century horror films still feed on the vampire myth.

people. It is an interesting coincidence that a common food containing a substance, which activates the haem-destroying enzyme, cytochrome P450 also happens to be a famous vampire-dispelling agent – garlic!

The true vampire (DESMODUS ROTUNDUS), a native of tropical America, is indeed a blood-drinking bat.

Historical Mysteries

✦

VOYNICH MANUSCRIPT

Amid the vast store of knowledge contained within the Beinecke Rare Book and Manuscript Library at Yale University is a unique medieval manuscript lavishly illustrated with colour paintings of strange plants and astronomical symbols, not to mention a varied selection of nude women. The only problem is that the ornate script of this book's 200-page text is written in a wholly unknown language that has withstood all attempts in modern times to decipher it.

This baffling tome is known as the Voynich Manuscript, named after New York book dealer Wilfred M. Voynich who purchased it in 1912 from the library of a Jesuit college in Frascati, Italy. Accompanying the manuscript was a letter dated 1666, written to the famous Jesuit scholar Athanasius Kircher by his former tutor Marcus Marci. In his letter, Marci claimed that the manuscript's author had been identified as Roger Bacon, an outstanding English scientist/alchemist from the thirteenth century, by one of the manuscript's previous owners, Holy Roman Emperor Rudolph II (died 1612).

After purchasing the manuscript, Voynich made copies available to many

of the world's leading code-breakers, including teams employed in wartime cypher interpretation, as well as ancient language researchers – but all to no avail. Not only is the language resolutely incomprehensible, most of the illustrated species of flowers do not even exist!

When Voynich's widow died in 1960,

Strange plants feature in the Voynich manuscript.

the manuscript was sold to book dealer Hans Kraus, whose attempts to market it ended in such disappointment that in 1969 he donated the exasperating tome to Yale University. Among the identities offered to explain it are that it represents an attempt to devise an artificial language, an extravagant hoax,

an example of spirit-mediated automatic writing or an exceedingly peculiar herbal catalogue.

The only person to achieve the slightest degree of success in exposing its secrets is Yale University's own Professor Robert S. Brumbaugh, who considers it to be an alchemical work; such works are well known for their elaborate symbolism and cryptic text. A few scribbled calculations in the manuscript's margins led him to formulating a code whereby he was able to decipher some of the names of those few illustrated plants in it that do exist, and also certain stars. Aside from that, the text's contents continue to remain a complete mystery.

I wonder if Yale University has considered the idea of self-publishing the Voynich Manuscript, selling it in their bookshops and any others willing to stock it, and announcing in a blaze of media publicity that a handsome prize will be given to anyone who succeeds in deciphering the manuscript and making their methods available for independent scrutiny? Bearing in mind Roger Bacon's fame for accurately predicting many major scientific inventions and principles centuries before they were conceived, however, perhaps some researchers have voiced the opinion that his extraordinary manuscript might well contain secrets that are best left undiscovered, even in this modern age.

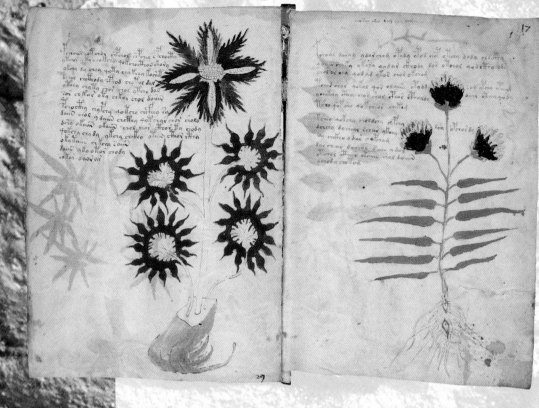

The Voynich manuscript, written in a wholly unknown language.

⬟ ATLAND – THE "OTHER" ATLANTIS

The mysterious Oera Linda Book chronicles the supposed history of a northern continent called Atland, wholly distinct from Atlantis but equally lost today. A semicircular land mass sited off the Netherlands' Frisian coast, idyllic Atland had a subtropical climate and contented people, until a great catastrophe in 2193 BC destroyed the island and many, but not all, of its inhabitants. Those who survived travelled elsewhere, establishing some of the world's most significant civilizations, including those of the ancient Egyptians, Greeks and Indians.

As if all of this were not sufficiently radical, other fascinating insights into the Atlandian era include the origin of its own civilization as an offshoot from that of Atlantis, destroyed several millennia earlier, Frisian heroes as the original models for the Norse deities, a visit to Atland by the Greek hero Ulysses (Odysseus), the development of our numerical symbols not from the Arabic but from ancient Frisian, and Atland's use of Britain as a penal colony!

If its contents are indeed true, the Oera Linda Book would require historians to rewrite considerable portions of humanity's history, so what is known about this revolutionary document's own history and origin? It first attracted modern-day attention in 1848 when a Frisian antiquarian called Cornelius Over de Linden (i.e. Oera Linda) showed the manuscript to Dr E. Verwijs, Librarian of the Provincial Library of Leeuwarden in Friesland. The manuscript, written on cotton paper using iron-free black ink, had supposedly been copied in 1256 from a previous version and had been in the Oera Linda family ever since.

Verwijs was keen to see the book published, but when he approached the Frisian Society to sponsor such an undertaking, it refused, condemning the work as a hoax. In 1876, however, an eminently respectable London publisher, Trubner & Co., did publish it, with the original Frisian script printed alongside an English version by William R. Sandbach (derived in turn from a Dutch translation, by Dr J. O. Ottema, of the Frisian). Not unexpectedly, however, historians were virtually unanimous in their opinion that the manuscript was a complete fraud, differing only in their ideas as to who was the perpetrator, with Cornelius Oera Linda, Verwijs, or both, among the leading contenders.

And there its history might well have ended – unknown, briefly revealed, then forgotten once more – had it not been for Robert J. Scrutton, who restored it to public attention via his own books, *The Other Atlantis* and *The Secrets of Lost Atland*. Nevertheless, the erstwhile existence of Atland and the pioneering activities of its survivors have still largely failed to gain any official acceptance, though a rare vote of support for them appears in *Unsolved Mysteries: Past and Present* by Colin and Damon Wilson.

Yet who can be surprised? Any work that overturns every traditional concept of human advancement, offering what is in effect an entirely alternative history of the world but with scant independent support for its claims, is unlikely to be enthusiastically received by the academic community. Even the

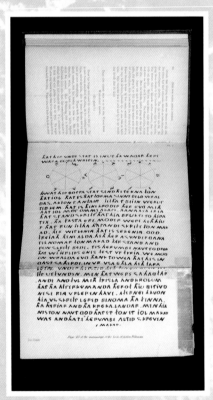

Part of the Oera Linda manuscript reproduced in the 1876 publication.

adherents of Immanuel Velikovsky's own highly individual, but exhaustively researched views of human history as expounded in *Worlds in Collision* and other works, are deeply suspicious of this book's authenticity – and they of all people might have been expected to show some sympathy for a work that challenges orthodox beliefs, had it shown any real promise of scholarly plausibility. So RIP Atland and the Oera Linda Book ... again.

✦

THE WANDERING JEW

During the Middle Ages, one of the most tenacious legends circulating through Europe was that of the Wandering Jew, Cartaphilus, originally employed as a porter by Pontius Pilate. According to the legend, after Pilate had delivered him to the Jews for crucifixion, Jesus was being dragged out of the judgement hall when he paused for a moment to rest. Seeing this, Cartaphilus cruelly struck him on the back with his hand and jeered, "Go quicker, Jesus, go quicker; why do you loiter?" In reply, Jesus looked back at the porter and said, "I am going, and you will wait till I return." (In some versions of the legend, Jesus was struck by Cartaphilus as he staggered past bearing his cross.) Since that day, Cartaphilus has roamed the world unceasingly, unable to die until the Last Judgement.

This stark tale was first documented in the book of the chronicles of the abbey at St Albans, England, which was copied and continued by Matthew Paris. He recorded that in AD 1228, the abbey was visited by a certain archbishop from Armenia, who told the monks that Cartaphilus had eaten at his table and that they had often spoken together. Apparently, he was now known as Joseph, following his baptism by Ananias (who also baptized the apostle Paul). A similar account of the Armenian archbishop's testimony was penned in 1242 by Philip Mouskes, who later became Bishop of Tournay.

During the sixteenth century, reports of the Wandering Jew were numerous and widespread. In 1505, he reputedly assisted a weaver called Kokot to find a

The Wandering Jew, from an illustration in **Le Juif Errant** *(1845).*

treasure that had been hidden in the royal palace in Bohemia 60 years earlier, during the Jew's previous visit there. Not long afterwards, he supposedly spoke with the Arab hero Fadhilah after the capture of the city of Elvan by the Arab. On that occasion, the Jew gave his name as Bassi Hadhret Issa.

During the winter of 1547, he was spied in a Hamburg church by a student called Paul von Eitzen, later to become Bishop of Schleswig. A tall man with long hair, despite the freezing weather the Jew was barefoot and dressed only in threadbare clothing, a description frequently given by eyewitnesses. Listening solemnly to the sermon, he

sighed and beat his breast whenever the name of Jesus was mentioned. Afterwards Eitzen sought him out, learning that he now called himself Ahasuerus, and listening in awe as the Jew regaled him with extensive details of his life and those of the countless famous people encountered by him during his unending travels. Again, the Jew's seemingly vast knowledge of history, as well as his ability to speak in many languages, was alluded to in numerous other eyewitness narratives too. Moreover, he never laughed, refused all offers of money or gifts, and harshly rebuked anyone speaking of God or Jesus in a blasphemous manner.

VERSAILLES TIME-SLIP

During the afternoon of 10 August 1901, two middle-aged English spinsters, college principal Charlotte "Annie" Moberly and headmistress Eleanor Jourdain, were walking through the gardens of the Palace of Versailles, seeking a building called the Petit Trianon. Looking around, they suddenly found that all the other people nearby seemed to be wearing strange clothes, resembling those worn in pre-Revolution France during the eighteenth century. On the steps of a summerhouse was a man, also dressed in this anachronistic style, whose face was visibly pockmarked by smallpox, which was common in the 1700s. And when they reached the Petit Trianon, Moberly (but not Jourdain) saw a woman in an elaborate eighteenth-century gown, who was sketching: the woman greatly resembled King Louis XVI's consort, Marie Antoinette!

The gardens at Versailles in the mid eighteenth century.

In their subsequent book, *An Adventure*, the two women expressed no doubt that they had either spied ghosts from the 1780s or had travelled back in time to that period. Other people came forward to announce that they too had experienced similar sights in the Versailles gardens. Moreover, schoolteacher Clare M. Burrow had allegedly walked through a gate here that was later shown to have been sealed up for over a century.

In *The Ghosts of the Trianon*, Michael H. Coleman concluded that the two women had probably come unsuspectingly upon a rehearsal for a theatrical pageant with actors in period costume, but how can that explain Miss Burrow's sealed gate? Similarly, the women claimed to have seen a plough, but were told by the gardeners that there was no plough in the gardens; such a plough did exist here, however, during the reign of Louis XVI. Is that just a coincidence, or do these gardens truly offer a window – even a doorway – into the past?

Eleanor Jourdain. *Charlotte Moberly.*

The Jew was supposedly seen by many people in Hamburg at that time, inspiring the German publication of a popular pamphlet outlining his history (a reflection of this period's anti-Semitism?) and also, much later, a series of dramatic wood-cuts by Gustave Doré.

In 1575, the secretary Christopher Krause and Master Jacob von Holstein, legates to the court of Spain, claimed to have met the Jew while travelling through Madrid. By the close of the century, he had also been reported from Vienna, from Cracow and Moscow in 1601, Lubeck in 1603, and Paris in 1604. By 1633 he was back in Hamburg, Brussels in 1640, Leipzig in 1642, Munich in 1721, and at the beginning of the 1800s he was travelling through Scandinavia. The most recent report comes from Salt Lake City, Utah, in 1868.

What are we to make of such a strange affair? Perhaps the most perceptive comment was made by John Allan in *Mysteries*: "... there is no shred of evidence for its truth. Apart from anything else, since Christ was prepared to forgive his killers as he hung on the cross, it seems monstrously out of character for him to condemn one man eternally for a single blow."

✷

THE PIED PIPER OF HAMELIN – FOLKLORE OR FACT?

The year was 1284, and the town of Hamelin in Lower Saxony, Germany, was besieged by a plague of rats. The despairing townsfolk offered a sizeable reward to anyone who could rid them of these rodents. One day a stranger arrived, dressed in garish two-tone attire, and by skilful playing of his musical pipe he lured the rats into the river Weser, where they all drowned. However, the ungrateful people refused to pay him his reward, so the piper began to play again, but this time it was not the rats but the town's own children who were called forth. Still playing, the sinister piper led 130 of them away, eastward out of Hamelin and on towards a hill called Koppen, which opened as they approached and closed up again when they had entered. Neither the piper nor the children were ever seen again.

There are many historians, especially in Germany, who believe that this famous fairy tale has a firm basis in fact. In Hamelin itself is a street called Bungelosen Strasse. This is the street through which the children supposedly ran when called by the piper's bewitching music; ever since, it has been forbidden by law to play any form of music here. It also bears an inscription recalling the piper's dreadful deed and fixing its date as 26 June 1284.

In 1982, Maurice Shadbolt revealed how, while investigating the pied piper myth at Hamelin, he visited the home of retired schoolteacher Hans Dobbertin, who has spent much of his life attempting to trace Hamelin's lost children and is now certain of their true fate. Dobbertin's theory hinges upon the key fact that in medieval times, German colonization of eastern territories was greatly encouraged, not only because they were eminently suitable for settlement, but also because their Slav and Hungarian overlords needed all the help they could obtain to prevent their lands from being overrun by the savage Tartars.

According to Dobbertin, the vanishing pied piper was most probably Count Nicholas von Spiegelberg, a German colonizer with longstanding connections in the Hamelin area. As for Hamelin's lost "children", Dobbertin and Shadbolt consider it much more likely that these were actually a group of disaffected teenagers, out of work and eager to make a new start elsewhere, who were encouraged by Spiegelberg to seek their fortune in the east of the country.

Dobbertin believes that Spiegelberg and the "children" journeyed north-east, eventually boarding a ship that sank, drowning everyone aboard, near a Pomeranian coastal village called Kopahn, now contained within Poland. He considers that over the course of several centuries, the name "Kopahn" became confused with that of "Koppen", the hill beyond Hamelin.

Spiegelberg was last seen on 8 July

The Pied Piper of Hamelin in an illustration by Arthur Rackham (1939).

1284, at the Baltic port of Stettin, several days' journey from Hamelin. Of particular note is that Stettin, like Kopahn, was a port along the route habitually taken by German colonizers travelling to the Baltic region. Even the piper's pied attire recalls the ornate outfits worn by German noblemen like Spiegelberg.

But what of the earlier portion of the legend, in which the piper rids Hamelin of its rats? Shadbolt believes this to be an entirely separate event. He claims that it was merely an example of rat removal involving the playing of a high-pitched tin whistle of the type frequently used for this purpose by

English rat-catchers; this was later erroneously tagged on to the tragic deaths of the town's teenagers when their ship sank near Kopahn. As a result, a wholly new story was created whose strange qualities have persisted long after the more prosaic reality had been forgotten.

Interestingly, a similar theory has been outlined by various other historians, but nominating Bishop Bruno of Olmütz (now Olomouc) as the piper figure, anxious to obtain colonizers for his diocese in Bohemia. They point out the many similarities in family names between the town records of Olomouc and Hamelin.

✵ WHATEVER HAPPENED TO THE LIZARD KING?

On 3 July 1971, Jim Morrison – lead singer with The Doors, and one of the world's most enigmatic rock stars – died of a heart attack in his bath. Or did he? Every year, fans old and new visit the Parisian cemetery of Père Lachaise, to see the grave in which he was buried. Or was he? For over 20 years, rumours have been circulating about the sensational possibility that the death of this mystical 1960s icon was a stage-managed sham – that in reality Jim shed his leather-clad

Memorial to Jim Morrison at Père Lachaise cemetery, Paris.

Lizard King persona and took on a new identity elsewhere.

Claims regarding this new identity are as varied as they are numerous, as reviewed in "Rumors, Myths and Urban Legends Surrounding the Death of Jim Morrison", an absorbing article by Thomas Lyttle in *Secret and Suppressed* (1993). Some of these stories tell of a mysterious businessman supposedly involved in banking transactions at San Francisco's Bank of America. Others allude to a frequenter of certain controversial bars and night-clubs in Los Angeles. Who is the secretive star of various radio programmes in Louisiana? Could Jim be a James-Bond-style intelligence agent with CIA links? According to yet another line of speculation, he is presently working as a minicab driver in Camberley!

Nevertheless, the concept of a faked death is not as outlandish as it might initially seem. Certainly, Jim was weary of his rock-star image, which he felt was responsible for his failure to achieve his aspired status as a serious poet. He had also publicly expressed a desire on many occasions to change his identity, to disappear and reappear as someone different.

But there is more to consider than just the necessary motive and inclination. Why was the media not informed of his death for six days – two days *after* the funeral itself? Isn't it rather strange that his parents were prevented from seeing his body, and that even his manager, the person who made the official announcement of his death, did not see it? Instead, he saw only Jim's widow Pamela, a sealed coffin (which a fellow Doors member claimed to be too small to hold Jim's tall body) and a death certificate made out by a local French doctor who has steadfastly refused to give interviews on the subject.

In addition, there was no autopsy of his body, the funeral was attended by just a few very close friends amid intense secrecy, and attempts since then by fans to obtain permission for the body to be dug up and formally examined have always been blocked. As for Pamela, the one person who would certainly know the truth, she died three years after Jim, without releasing any information.

Even those who accept that Jim's death was genuine are in disagreement

about its precise nature. Some discount a heart attack in preference for such diverse alternatives as: a drug overdose; assassination by covert intelligence agencies in the USA or France; death via spider venom used in magic initiation rituals, Jim was fascinated by many forms of occult practices, particularly voodoo; and supernatural murder via long-distance witchcraft perpetrated by a jilted lover in New York!

Thomas Lyttle offered a thought-provoking opinion from Ray Manzarek, keyboard player with The Doors: "If there was one guy that would have been capable of staging his own death – getting a phony death certificate and paying off some French doctor ... And putting a hundred and fifty pound sack of sand into a coffin and splitting to some point on this planet – Africa, who knows where – it is Jim Morrison who would have been able to pull it off."

Jim was famous for his macabre sense of humour: did he have the last laugh after all?

✵ STRANGE MUSIC

Certain famous European songs have some very strange tales to tell, far stranger than any of their lyrics, but few are more unnerving than the history of the song "Gloomy Sunday".

It was written in Paris one rainy Sunday in December 1932 by the Hungarian composer Reszo Seress, on the day after his girlfriend had ended their engagement. Intensely depressed, Seress was contemplating just how very gloomy this particular Sunday was when a hauntingly sad tune that was totally unknown to him began to play in his mind. Shocked out of his despair by this unexpected event, Seress jotted down the tune and entitled it "Gloomy Sunday". The words that he penned for it told the tragic story of a man whose lover had recently died and who was now considering suicide in order to be united with her again.

The first publishers to whom Seress took "Gloomy Sunday" turned it down, claiming it to be too melancholy. Indeed, one of them felt that it might be better if people never heard it. This opinion proved to be very prophetic, for once the song was published its unrelentingly sad strain soon gained a notorious reputation for inciting people to commit suicide.

The first known instance occurred in spring 1933, when a youth sitting in a Budapest cafe asked the band to play "Gloomy Sunday". After they had finished playing it, he promptly went home and shot himself. In a chilling account of this song's dark history by Tane Jackson in *The Unknown* (May 1987), several other alleged cases are given, though no names of the people concerned are mentioned, testifying to the fatal attraction of "Gloomy Sunday". Its victims even included singers who had incorporated its deadly refrain in their repertoires.

In one of the most disturbing cases, a London flat was broken into by neighbours after hearing the mournful melody of "Gloomy Sunday" playing incessantly inside. There they found the flat's owner, a young woman, lying dead on the floor from an overdose, with a gramophone endlessly playing the fatal song.

By the late 1930s, "Gloomy Sunday" had incited such a degree of public alarm that the Hungarian government discouraged public performances of it. Needless to say, this came as a great relief to many musicians, who had seriously begun to fear for their own continued well-being whenever they had to play Seress's uncanny composition. Many radio stations, including the BBC, considered banning it (a number of local stations in the USA did refuse to play it), and several families of suicide victims whose deaths were linked to this sinister song (over 200 in total) attempted unsuccessfully to ban it entirely.

The English version of "Gloomy Sunday" was written by Sam Lewis, and in 1941 a record of it was released by Billie Holliday. By then, however, the song's notoriety had lessened: with the coming of the Second World War there were many far more dramatic events to engage popular attention. Even so, its malign influence had not entirely ceased.

Gordon Beck, of Salisbury in Wiltshire, who served with 76 Squadron at RAF Yeravda in Poona, India, during 1946, recently recalled how one of his

The composer Tartini receives diabolic inspiration in this contemporary engraving.

fellow pilots would become very upset if ever he heard him playing his record of "Gloomy Sunday" (a version by the Artie Shaw Orchestra, with a female vocalist), the pilot claiming that it made him feel suicidal. Beck thought little of this, until he began flying too and discovered to his alarm that he could not get the song's haunting melody out of his head; it penetrated his mind even above the noise of the aeroplane's engines. Never again did Beck play "Gloomy Sunday".

How can the disturbing effect of this eerie song be explained? Perhaps, as suggested by Tane Jackson, Seress had expressed his own profound emotions of grief so successfully in the song that it somehow amplifies those of people listening to it who are similarly depressed, inducing them to take their own lives as a means of escaping their sadness. This disturbing prospect is not as unlikely as it might seem. In *The Secret Power of Music*, David Tame reveals that music can exert some astounding effects upon humans, influencing stress, heart rate, digestion and other metabolic processes, as well as our emotional and mental well-being.

Perhaps the most poignant cases

linked with "Gloomy Sunday" are those of the two people who were responsible for its creation. Its composer, Reszo Seress, committed suicide in 1968 by leaping off a building, after confessing that he had never been able to write another hit song. As for the girl who had jilted him all those years ago, she had already been found dead, alongside a sheet of paper on which she had written the words "Gloomy Sunday".

Another supposedly unlucky song is "I Dreamt That I Dwelt in Marble Halls", from Rudolf Friml's operetta *The Bohemian Girl*. Believed to bring bad luck to anyone who hears it, this song stirs up much the same feeling of dread among singers (some of whom perform it only with great reluctance) as the Shakespearean play *Macbeth* does among actors, who prefer to call it simply "the Scottish Play". Yet no one seems to know how or why this song gained its ill-starred reputation.

Some songs, rather like "Gloomy Sunday", seem to be written by the subconscious rather than the conscious mind. One night while asleep, the Italian composer Guiseppe Tartini dreamed that the devil was playing an exquisite tune to him on a violin. Waking up,

THE OUROBOUROS OF ORGANIC CHEMISTRY

One of the most famous aromatic compounds in organic chemistry is benzene, whose molecules each consist of six carbon atoms and six hydrogen atoms: but what is benzene's molecular structure? Today, the answer to this question is well known, but during much of the nineteenth century it was a profound mystery.

One night, after yet another fruitless attempt to discover the structure, German chemist Friedrich August Kekulé fell asleep and dreamed a bizarre dream in which the various atoms of benzene were cavorting all around him, combining and recombining in a dizzy phantasmagoria of shapes. Suddenly, right before his amazed eyes, they united to form an ourobouros – a snake-like dragon that clasps its own tail in its mouth, forming a ring. Instantly, Kekulé awoke and knew that at last he had found the answer: the six carbon atoms of benzene were linked to one another not in a line, or in a series of branched connections, but in a closed ring! And he was right.

Tartini attempted to write down the tune from his dream, and although he claimed that the result was greatly inferior, it became his most famous work – "The Devil's Trill". Similarly, in *Yesterday and Today*, Ray Coleman revealed that one late morning in 1963, the tune for what was destined to be one of the world's most frequently recorded songs came to its composer in a dream. The composer was Paul McCartney, and the song was "Yesterday".

✦

COUNT ST GERMAIN

Count St Germain is surely the quintessential "man of mystery". Although he was well-acquainted with many of the most eminent figures of eighteenth-century Europe, no one knew anything about him. His real name, his origin, background, the source of his inestimable wealth, even his age – all were shrouded in controversy, which he made no attempt to dispel.

He first came to attention in 1710, when seen in Venice by a youthful Countess von Georgy, who estimated him to be 45–50 years old. She saw him again in the late 1750s, only to discover that he did not look a day older than when she had first met him in Venice.

From 1737 until 1784, he travelled widely through Europe and beyond, visiting and offering (with varied degrees of success) all manner of advice and assistance to King Louis XV of France and other leading figures of the day. In 1743 his arrival at Versailles was a sensation, with countless stories and rumours circulating about this exotic-looking stranger, garbed in the most expensive clothes and literally dripping with spectacular diamonds – festooning his fingers, filling his pockets, and used by him in preference to money.

As the years passed by, the mysteries surrounding this charismatic count grew ever stranger. He refused to eat in public. He claimed to have lived for untold centuries and to have personally encountered the Holy Family. He was a welcomed member of many of the most esoteric occult societies. When asked about his immense wealth he spoke of how he had attained the alchemists' fabled philosopher's stone for converting base metals into gold, hinted of secret processes for creating enormous diamonds, of studies conducted in the Egyptian pyramids and meetings with the learned mystics of the Himalayas. He was said to possess healing powers,

Count St Germain – master alchemist or artful charlatan?

to undergo out-of-the-body journeys, and he visibly trembled with fear before fleeing from the room when, on one occasion, he was referred to as a devil. He even claimed to possess the alchemical elixir of eternal life – and it was not just his stories and his never-ageing appearance that gave people reason to believe this.

On 27 February 1784, Count St Germain died. He was buried at Eckernförde in Germany on 2 March, but not even death, it seemed, could suppress this irrepressible enigma for long. In 1785, he (or someone exactly like him) made a well-attested appearance at an occult conference in Wilhelmsbad. In future years he was seen many times – with fellow occultists, or advising Marie Antoinette, or visiting Sweden's King Gustavus III and many others too.

Even the twentieth century may not have escaped his personal attention. In January 1972, a Parisian man called Richard Chanfray, ostensibly in his mid-40s and claiming to be the count, appeared on television, and with the aid of a camping stove performed what seemed to be a successful transmutation of lead into gold. In November 1992, veteran traveller Douchan Gersi claimed to have met a mysterious person in Haiti called St Germain, who dematerialized in Gersi's hotel room, 100 miles away from Port-au-Prince, then reappeared 32 minutes later holding a book that Gersi had left behind in another hotel – at Port-au-Prince.

The saga of Count St Germain is a strange story indeed, inviting comparisons with figures from the past and the future, from fiction and from fact – Baron Munchausen and the Wandering Jew, Faust and Fulcanelli, with even a dash of Dorian Gray thrown in for good measure. Was Count St Germain simply a smooth-talking charlatan, or a master alchemist who had achieved occult successes far beyond the dreams of science? Do the recent incidents merely indicate that the romance of the count's cryptic history has inspired a modern-day generation of pretenders to his throne, or is it conceivable that the twentieth century has indeed witnessed the latest activities of the genuine article? Of course, they say that old legends die hard, but then again, so too do old habits ...

THE PROPHECIES OF NOSTRADAMUS

In print for over 500 years, and second, therefore, only to the Bible for continuous publication, are the prophecies of a sixteenth-century French seer from Saint-Rémy called Michel de Notredame, better known to the world as Nostradamus. Supporters are convinced that he has accurately predicted many significant events in Europe, and elsewhere too, including Hitler's invasion of Poland, the Great Fire of London and the recent civil war in Yugoslavia. Sceptics consider that any such "accuracies" merely reflect the great influence of hindsight upon the prophecies' translators and the interpretations of these translations.

PORTRAIT DE MICHEL NOSTRADAMUS, Astronome célèbre.

The fundamental problem lies in the fact that in order to avoid possible accusations of witchcraft, Nostradamus deliberately concealed his predictions' true meaning in a welter of obscurity. They comprise 965 quatrains penned in a cryptic mixture of Latin, Greek, French and his native Provençal, their wording is purposely ambiguous and contains numerous invented words that do not exist elsewhere, and the time-sequence of the quatrains is not ordered.

Inevitably, the translations and interpretations differ greatly: a given quatrain can yield several wholly separate predictions. Even one of the more lucid examples, referring to a devastation of London's people by thunderbolts, has been variously interpreted as foretelling the burning of martyrs by Queen Mary I, the Great Fire of London or the Blitz in 1940.

Among the delights predicted by Nostradamus for the end of the twentieth century were another world war (which Europe would lose), and European decimation by a terrible plague. Thankfully, neither of these chilling prophecies came true!

✦

THE SMILE ON THE FACE OF THE MONA LISA

For many people, Leonardo da Vinci's world-famous painting, "The Mona Lisa", is simply a portrait of the wife of Francesco del Giocondo, a wealthy Florentine merchant. Certain investigators, conversely, claim that her enigmatic smile hides some startling surprises.

Why, for instance, is this particular painting so alluring? Dr Leopold Bellak, a psychology professor at New York University, has analysed her face using the Zone System, whereby the left and right sides are studied independently, as are the top and bottom halves. Bellak concludes that her full cheeks suggest sensual indulgence and her weak chin implies a lack of self-control – flirtatious enough, perhaps, to attract the eye of any red-blooded male?

Perhaps not. As revealed by Tim Walker in an excellent review of Mona Lisa mysteries (*Daily Mail*, 21 October 1993), American computer artist Lillian Schwartz and Maudsley Hospital registrar Dr Digby Quested believe that her face yields a very different message – for they claim that it is actually a mirror image of Leonardo da Vinci's own face!

Although it is known that Leonardo penned many notes in mirror-image writing, the concept of a transvestite Mona Lisa is still something of a shock; but worse is to come. The picture was stolen from the Louvre in 1911, and when later recovered it was X-rayed to check its authenticity. That was confirmed, but the X-rays also revealed that the Mona Lisa had apparently possessed a beard at one time, which had later been painted over.

If the Mona Lisa is a disguised portrait of Leonardo, however, then he may well have been even more remarkable a man than hitherto supposed. According to Dr Kenneth Keale, a consultant at Ashford Hospital, Middlesex, her cheery smile, youthful complexion, generous body proportions and the way in which her robe falls into her lap all show that the person depicted in this painting is heavily pregnant!

Pregnancies aside, she (or he?) may not have been in the best of health when posing for the portrait. In the view of Californian medical specialist Dr Kedar Ardour, her captivating smile is in fact the result of a type of facial paralysis called Bell's palsy, which explains its lop-sided shape. This is aided and abetted, according to Maryland dentist Dr Joseph Borkowski, by the equally tragic fact that she had somehow lost her front teeth, which is why her lips droop at the corners. But before we lose sight altogether of the mystique associated with the Mona Lisa, we should perhaps be thankful that the portrait was ever painted at all. In the opinion of Japanese heart specialist Dr Haruo Nakamura, noting the yellow pigmentation in the corner of her left eye, the person posing for this picture possessed high cholesterol levels and could have suffered a heart attack at any moment. So much for the healthy foods of earlier ages!

Mona Lisa, painted by Leonardo da Vinci c. 1503. Is this in fact a disguised portrait of the artist?

✸ KASPAR HAUSER

As far as the rest of the world is concerned, Kaspar Hauser literally stepped into existence on 26 May 1828 when, as an incoherent 16- or 17-year-old, he staggered into Nuremberg's Unschlitt Square, wearing expensive but tattered clothing and ill-fitting boots, and clutching an envelope addressed to "the Captain of the 4th Squadron, 6th Cavalry Regiment".

Taken there by a cobbler who had spotted him, he handed his envelope to the captain, who found that it contained two letters. These stated that throughout his life he had been locked away from the outside world and contact with other humans, and that he should now be trained as a cavalry soldier like his father. Reacting in a bizarre manner to inanimate objects such as a clock and a candle flame, which he seemed to believe were alive, and dismissed by the captain as a simpleton, he was taken to the police station, but when given a pen and paper he wrote "Kaspar Hauser". This was assumed by everyone to be his name.

Attempts were made to teach Kaspar to talk, read and write, and he responded with astonishing speed, becoming fluent in all three within just a few weeks. He confirmed that he had spent his entire life imprisoned in a darkened place, sleeping or sitting on straw and tended to by persons unseen, yet he seemed remarkably healthy under the circumstances. In August 1829, Kaspar's autobiography was published, but it contained no new details about his past and was not a success. Shortly afterwards, however, he hit the headlines when on 7 October he suffered a mysterious wound to his brow, which he said had been inflicted by a man with "a black face" (a mask?). Yet no one else had seen such a person.

During the next few years Kaspar toured Europe in the company of Lord Stanhope, an English aristocrat, but his life was soon to come to a highly controversial end. On 14 December 1833, at Ansbach near Nuremberg, Kaspar stumbled into the house of a local teacher called Dr Meyer, bleeding from a severe stab wound in his chest and claiming to have been attacked in the park. He showed Meyer a wallet supposedly given to him by his attacker immediately before the incident, which contained a meaningless message in mirror writing. Yet when the police went to the site of the incident, only Kaspar's footprints could be found.

Monument erected to the memory of Kasper Hauser, a youth without a past.

On 17 December, Kaspar died, avowing to the end that the wounds were not self-inflicted.

Over 150 years of speculation have failed to shed any light upon his identity, his strange claims and behaviour, or the significance of the two attacks. Was Kaspar a fraud who enjoyed the glamour that his stories had brought for him in Nuremberg, or was he an equivalent of sorts to the many "feral children" who have survived in the wild without any human parental care? If the latter is true, how can his amazingly swift understanding of reading and writing be explained, and what was the reason for his years of isolation? Were his "attacks" self-inflicted, to maintain public interest in him, or could they have been sinister attempts to silence him by those who feared what he may reveal as he became more articulate?

Kaspar Hauser was buried beneath a headstone that spoke only of a youth without a past, who was robbed of a future. Such is the sum total of our knowledge concerning one of the most enigmatic figures from modern times.

Kaspar Hauser as portrayed in the **Magasin Pittoresque** *in 1837.*

INDEX

Picture Credits

About the Author

Dr Karl P.N. Shuker is a zoologist, lecturer and writer who specializes in cryptozoology and animal mythology. A scientist with a longstanding interest in unexplained phenomena of all kinds, Dr Shuker has amassed a considerable archive of material during many years of personal research. He is a regular contributor to *Strange*, America's most credible magazine dedicated to exploring unexplained phenomena. Dr Shuker's books include *The Lost Ark: New and Rediscovered Animals of the 20th Century*, and *Mystery Cats of the World*. He acted as consultant to Reader's Digest on *Almanac of the Uncanny*; *Secrets of the Natural World*; *Man and Beast* and to Guinness on the *Guinness Book of Records*.